Play and Learning for the Under 3's

JENNIE LINDON
KEVIN KELMAN
ALICE SHARP

Play and Learning for the Under 3's

Senior Editor Jennifer Siklós
Assistant Editor Edward FitzGerald

Commissioning Editor Patricia Grogan

Art Editor Nicola Liddiard

Photography Andy Crawford

Additional Photography Tony Stone picture agency

First published in Great Britain in 2001 by
TSL Education Limited,
Admiral House, 66–68 East Smithfield, London E1W 1BX

A CIP catalogue record for this book is available from the British Library

ISBN 1-84122-010-8

Printed and bound in Belgium by Proost

In memory of David Purcell

a time of learning

Babies and toddlers are primed to learn and recent research into the development of the human brain has shown the importance of this early potential. The babies' efforts within their early, all-round development stimulate the possible neural networks within their immature brains. These networks then develop into actual physical connections that support further learning. Within the first two or three years of life, more connections in total can be made than are created at any other time of our life. This research confirms what involved practitioners and parents have always said: that the early years are a time of great potential. However, such possibilities can be lost if parents and other carers relate poorly to babies and toddlers, or if we channel the play and learning experience of babies or toddlers in a very narrow way, inappropriate to their development.

The difference between a young baby and a three year old is visible and striking. If all has gone well, they have learned a tremendous amount within these few years. From helpless, completely dependent babies, young children have become individuals in their own right and are mobile, communicative, able to share in their own care and with interests and concerns of their own.

Undoubtedly there are many individual differences between even very young children and firm developmental expectations are not useful. However, realistic expectations, based on reliable information about development, are important if you are neither to underestimate children nor expect too much. Babies vary considerably, but they still have more in common with other babies than, for instance, with three year olds. Throughout this book you will therefore find sections called 'developmental focus', to support you in adjusting activities for a child's age and likely learning.

A positive outlook on very young children

Under threes are interesting in their own right

You need to focus on the babies and toddlers at the present, rather than on developmental 'milestones' that are weeks and months into the future.

- Appreciate the babies and toddlers as they are now: what they can manage and what they can nearly do, what they find fascinating and the ways in which they relate to the world. What they are learning is important for itself and not just for what will happen later.
- If you are alert to all the exciting smaller changes and learning, the baby and toddler will learn more easily and your day with them will be so much more interesting and satisfying.
- Get into the habit of 'baby watching' and notice what individual babies and toddlers do and how they do it. Keep notes as appropriate so that you can share your observations with parents and you can all look back with interest.

Value care and caring

Under threes do not split up their day into separate compartments, nor did they ever choose to have the care-education split that undermines our early years services.

- Care and caring matter a very great deal to very young children. They appreciate and are warmed by personal and respectful attention to their physical needs.
- Babies and toddlers will learn more easily in an environment where care matters and is never seen as somehow second best to 'educational' activities, however those are defined.
- Caring routines can be valuable times for warm communication and developing a close relationship between baby and carer.
- Value how much very young children can learn as you attend to their physical care or involve them in simple domestic routines.

Relax with children — you have time

Admittedly, some days can seem very full and busy but it is possible to become more harassed than necessary by losing your perspective on how very young children learn.

- The early years are indeed a window of opportunity but only if caring adults go at the child's pace and in tune with child's interests. Children switch off learning if they are pressurised and constantly directed by what adults think they ought to be learning now.
- Value the opportunities within caring and everyday routines. Do not dismiss them as something to get through in order to move on to apparently more valuable activities.
- You and the children have time: to relish activities, to do them again, to stop and look and just to be together.

Flexible planning

It is useful to have plans for each day and young children like some sense of routine.

- You need to look at a baby's or toddler's day as a whole and not as a list of separate activities.
- By all means plan ahead for a week

and the separate days. But then go with the flow each day of what interests the children. Be ready to pause and to follow a child's lead.

- Look towards what works well in family life. Home-based learning is a more flexible and developmentally appropriate model for very young children than more structured nursery programmes. (There is, of course, concern that some over threes are being pushed into inappropriately formal and highly planned days.)
- Young children relish a blend of novelty and familiarity. They enjoy new experiences, but they also learn from recognising a play activity or local outing. Sometimes the best choice for learning is 'let's do it again!'

Enjoy – you do not always have to make something

Older babies and toddlers like hands-on activities, such as play dough, simple sticking and drawing.

- Enjoy the activity with the toddlers and do not be concerned whether something emerges that can be a display. Enjoyable learning will often leave a happy memory, rather than an end product like a picture or model.
- Share with parents how much the children enjoyed the finger painting or how they have learned to use a thick crayon.
- Be careful not to push very young children into making something just because you feel a pressure to show an item to parents at the end of the day.

Caring adults count more than equipment

Think of yourself as the most vital item of play equipment in your nursery or home setting.

- If you relate warmly to babies and toddlers, they will learn supported within that relationship. On the other hand, when adults are uninvolved or uninterested in babies and toddlers, then good play equipment cannot make up that loss.
- Try to see the world through their eyes and hear with their ears. They have so much to learn and what is obvious to you may be intriguing or puzzling to them.
- Be close to very young children and at their visual level. Make it easy for them to engage with you.
- Be enthusiastic about activities with the children, be a part of what they do. If you are genuinely interested, children are more likely to learn.

Balance safety with interest

Babies and toddlers have no sense of danger and their natural curiosity can take them into trouble.

- They need your keen eye for their safety. But look for ways to meet their curiosity rather than limit them to a safe but boring world.
- If you are closely engaged with them, you can keep very young children safe by gentle intervention that does not disrupt

their play.

■ Any setting should remove obvious hazards and avoid the preventable accidents. However, babies and toddlers will not be able to learn if adults are so concerned about a long list of what could go wrong that they remove anything of interest.

Important note:
All the ideas within this book assume that adults will be attentive and closely involved in children's play and learning. None are intended as something you set out and then leave young children to complete on their own. Our assumption is that a caring and interested adult will always be very close to babies and toddlers. Although some suggestions have additional safety reminders, this general comment applies to everything that follows.

How to use this book

The book is organised into three main age sections:
Under twelve months;
From one to two years;
From two to three years.

This organisation will help you to choose activities that are more suitable to younger or older children. The sections should be treated flexibly. Some older babies are ready for a few of the toddler activities and three or even four year olds will still enjoy some of the ideas first introduced for younger ones. The sections can also be used to adjust to the developmental stage of a child who is older, but whose learning disabilities mean that appropriate activities are those more usually offered to younger children. Disabled children can sometimes get bored because of repetition within their choice for activities. So a resource of ideas at a similar developmental stage can be valuable.

There are five broad theme areas that are repeated within each age section:
Developing relationships: physical care and social development;
Using the senses: vision, touch, smell and hearing;
Language and creative development: early communication, arts and crafts, music, stories;
Physical development: gross and fine motor skills;
Using the environment: outdoor play, water and trips out.

This pattern will enable you to select ideas to cover the full range of children's interests and development. Similar ideas can, of course, promote children's learning and enthusiasm in more than one area. So some activities are revisited in different ways. The aim is that you use this material as a resource, to draw on and re-organise as suits the children and your setting. It is not intended that you treat any section as an inflexible programme to be done with the children from beginning to end.

Development within the first year

If all goes well, a very great deal happens within a baby's first twelve months. Their development is very dependent initially on the responsiveness of their carers. Babies learn within affectionate and close relationships with a small number of carers, including their parents, who take the time to know this very young person as an individual.

Undoubtedly young babies do sleep for many hours in total but that still leaves waking times in which they enjoy company and increasingly want to be entertained. Some babies have long wakeful periods from the early months and carers need a range of ideas and the willingness to chat with and carry around babies who simply do not want to be left alone.

Babies' interests and skills will build towards the more recognisable milestones, such as the 'first word' or 'first steps', so long as you value all the finer developments on the way. The first gestures and meaningful looks are forms of early communication and vital if recognisable words are to emerge later. A great deal of exciting physical movement and practice happens long before the first tottering steps and you will find life far more interesting with babies if you are attuned to what is happening day by day.

Learning to control their own limbs and whole body is a major focus for babies. Watch how much effort they put into the fine and larger movements and how hard they will try again and again to grab that interesting rattle or to get moving as a crawler. Mobility is a big issue, Once a baby becomes confident and is mobile, this opens up a whole new world for him. Even being able to sit without falling over, means that the baby has her hands free to play and explore.

Babies need a great deal of physical care for their health, growth and well being. However, physical caring also contributes to vital, close relationships between baby and carer and to the baby's sense of self worth when she is treated with patience and respect. Caring routines can and should be social times and opportunities for baby and carer to get to know each other better.

Babies do not make any distinction between learning and playing. They learn through what engages their interest and is supported by caring adults, whom they trust. Once you acknowledge that babies can learn through everything in which they participate, there will be no need to create special experiences or 'educational' activities. Babies and young children learn a great deal through happy involvement in the normal routines of their day and such events have meaning for them. In the following section you will find ideas for games with babies, but also many reminders of how to support their learning through what will be happening in the natural course of your time with them.

Contents

10–14 Developing relationships

15–24 Using the senses

25–33 Language and creative development

34–38 Physical development

39–43 Using the environment

developing relationships

Caring for babies – caring about babies

Developmental focus

A new-born baby has many basic needs for nutrition, sleep, warmth and cleanliness which have to be met for growth and development. All of these needs can be met through daily routines throughout the first year.

Feeding, changing and dressing a baby are ideal opportunities for sharing time, building relationships and offering experiences which support development and well-being. Some early years professionals are only too quick to dismiss physical care as a boring routine to get out of the way before finding some time left for 'educational' activities. Phrases like 'just care', and 'babies don't do anything!' are unfortunate and mistaken. Such attitudes are negative and disheartening, since they will block babies' development.

Yet physical care is an ideal vehicle for a great deal of learning. And babies who feel relaxed and have not been hustled through care routines, will be far more ready to enjoy everything else that is on offer in your setting. Key worker systems are crucial if adults are to learn a baby's personal preferences. Babies should feel cherished by one, or at most two, individual adults whom they get to recognise and trust. Dressing and feeding can support babies because they feel valued. Through affectionate and respectful touch you are telling them 'I care about you as well as care for you'. Good physical care, when you focus on the baby and give her your full attention, supports her personal and emotional development.

Play and learning tips

You need to value physical care as an ideal time for babies to learn.

Babies benefit from regular yet flexible care routines, that treat them as individuals and not just little bodies without a personality of their own. Avoid fixed routines in which babies are fed, put to rest or changed because it is time by the daily schedule. Staff should always ask themselves questions like, 'Is this baby hungry', or, 'does this baby need changing?'

Good communication with parents is important. You are sharing the care of their babies who need continuity between the important adults in their lives. Talk with parents about the baby's preferred routines, changes that a parent has made at home and what you have noticed in your setting.

Activities

Feeding

■ Hold babies securely yet gently when you are bottle feeding. Talk softly offering encouragement and gentle words of affection.

■ When winding, sit baby upright or place gently over your shoulder. Chat, whisper words of affirmation or softly pat her.

■ If an older baby is sitting in a suitable chair and is eating solids, allow her to watch you stirring, spooning and offering the food. This will become part of the baby's routine. Talk through the routine or repeat a little rhyme to tie in with it.

■ Focus on the baby; it's her mealtime. Talk and smile directly to her. (Avoid the bad habit of talking to other adults over the top of babies, whether feeding, cleaning or changing).

■ Encourage attempts to hold feeding utensils by offering objects for each hand, such as an empty bowl and spoon or two spoons. Allow the baby to experiment with them, moving them up and down, perhaps mirroring you.

■ Stimulate use of fingers and the development of hand-mouth co-ordination by playing games with the baby. First lift one of baby's hands to your mouth then to her own, doing the same with the other hand. Blow gently on the hand as a reward.

Changing and dressing

■ Use this personal time for friendly physical contact.

■ Touch, caress, stroke and tickle the baby while changing.

■ Blow gently on her hands and feet, arms and legs or tickle her palms, tummy and chin.

■ While developing this intimacy, talk quietly to her, repeat her name or the parts of the body you are touching.

■ Stretch her legs into the air, gently tap her feet together. Stretch her arms, gently tap her hands together. Play 'Round and round the garden' or 'This little piggy'.

■ While dressing her, play a game. 'Where's Anna's hand? Here it comes, here it comes!' or say a little rhyme, for example: 'Blue socks, red socks. Cover up your toes. Green socks, white socks. Warm and cosy toes'.

■ Put the baby's socks on your ears or trousers on your head to make her giggle.

■ Once fully clothed, gently roll the baby around the mat, or on the floor.

Keeping clean

■ Gently move baby through the water in the bath. Support her firmly and safely with one hand. With the other, trickle water over her tummy, chest and legs.

- Encourage the baby to move her legs and arms in the water, splashing her hands, fingers and feet.
- Lift your hands and allow the water to drain between your fingers. Support the baby in doing this too.
- Allow her to hold a small piece of soap, letting it slide and splash. Then pass her a toy, a small duck or ball which will float in the water.
- Use a sieve to create a bath shower. Hold the sieve over the baby's legs, pour a little water, then gradually add more.
- Wrap the baby in a warm, soft towel. While you are drying, play peek-a-boo with the towel. Say 'Where is Gemma, oh there she is, where is her hand? Toes? Tummy?' When each named part is uncovered, tickle that part gently.
- Wash and dry the baby's face while saying a rhyme, for example: 'Eye, nose, cheeky, cheeky, chin, cheeky, cheeky, chin, nose, eye.'

Sleep and rest time

- Lie quietly beside the baby on a comfortable mat or blanket. Chat, tickle and stroke him gently.
- Play at baby hugs. Gently lift the baby to you and hug him. Stretch your arms out, then bring him back towards you for a hug. Repeat a few times, placing your cheek against him.
- Dance gently while walking with him in your arms, hug him, and let him see you smile. Twirl slowly around and repeat.

Affectionate relationships

Developmental focus

Babies are primed and ready to become social beings. They stare intently at human faces, and strive for close physical contact. They want the reassuring sounds and scents of another human body to become familiar to them. Babies need to become closely attached to parents and to build affectionate relationships with other members of the family and one or two other key carers, if they have them. The security and trust that evolves with these attachments builds the basis for later social development.

Babies, and toddlers, need to form close attachments for healthy development. They cannot be 'too attached' to adults who are key in the babies' daily lives. So, they should be encouraged to develop attachments to their key worker. Adults, both workers and parents, need to resolve the mixed feelings that undoubtedly exist in this situation. Parents who work long hours may be uneasy that their baby is very fond of his key worker. But these understandable feelings need to be discussed between the adults and not 'solved' by making it hard for young children to form attachments in out-of-home care. Trying to stop babies and toddlers becoming 'too attached' is likely to disrupt their emotional and social development.

Play and learning tips

Organise the day so that babies are in contact with a key worker and perhaps one other familiar person. Make it easy for them to get to know you.

Talk with and listen to parents. Reassure them that babies can and do form attachments to more than one person. Let parents know when babies missed them or were happy to see them come back in at the end of the day. Invite parents to share something of their time with the baby.

Babies are interested in other babies and slightly older children so long as they are not rushed or required to be friendly to unfamiliar people.

Care in a family home can bring babies into relaxed contact with older children – look for ways in a nursery to bring the age groups together for at least some of the day.

Babies like to play repetitive games in which they have a role different from that of the adult or older child. Be patient and play the same game as often as the baby enjoys.

Make personal contact

- Hold very young babies close and share a warm mutual gaze. Talk to babies as individuals who matter to you. Join in the smiles when they come and touch babies gently on the face or hands.
- Greet babies when they wake or when you first see them. Let them know that you notice them, when they have woken from sleep and when they leave to go home.

Babies are individuals

- Babies will learn later about being part of a social group. For now, they are treated only as an individual. So look for any preferences that this baby shows about how he likes to be treated.
- Notice whether a baby shows special interest in one song rather than another. Does he like to stare at this particular picture or wall poster? Does one baby like a game in which you wiggle his toes but another baby likes to be bounced gently on your lap?
- Use the valuable time of physical care to look at babies and to communicate with them. Find a personal ritual that is slightly different for each baby in your care. Perhaps it is a special funny face you make or a rhyme that particularly makes this baby smile.
- Help babies to begin to distinguish the familiar from the unfamiliar by having a key worker system in a nursery. This means that the same person, or no more than two familiar carers, deals with babies' personal needs from day to day.
- Help the baby to recognise and relate to you by making full use of all his early skills of communication. Look closely at his face, make sounds and simple words, wait for his reply and encourage the turn-taking that is a source of pleasure in early social interactions.
- Follow the baby's sounds and faces as much as he follows yours.

Help babies to make contact

- Make it easy for slightly older babies (about four to twelve months) to watch what is going on as well as to explore their own suitable play materials. Make sure that their baby seat is placed so that they can watch you or other children.

■ Provide a safe base for babies to watch what's happening around them. Sit on the floor and have babies on your lap, sitting within your crossed legs or leaning against your body.

■ Watch as babies crawl off or toddle away to explore. Wave to them and greet them with, 'You're back!' as they return.

■ Babies are often enchanted by the attention of older children. Slightly older boys and girls are often adept at entertaining younger ones with the kind of repetitive games and sound plays that babies love.

■ By seven to eight months, babies can sit safely with their hands free to enjoy the contents of a treasure basket (see page 16). Two babies sitting at the basket will enjoy watching each other and may start to offer items to each other.

■ Take a moment to watch when older babies are trying to make contact. They use pats and prods that may sometimes unintentionally hurt the younger ones.

■ If necessary, show babies how to be more gentle in their body grasps and semi-wrestling. Only step in to help babies soften their grasp rather than assuming that the intention is to hurt. Gently unloose a firm grip on someone's hair or ear.

All a game

■ Play interactive games when the baby gives you a toy and then immediately takes it back again or when they drop or throw a toy that you fetch. Join in the fun with warm remarks like, 'But I thought that was for me!' or, 'How many more times?'

■ Look for games that a baby develops and respond with enjoyment. One baby might relish holding down the page of the board book just as you are about to turn it. Another baby might love pointing to parts of the room and getting you to look. Yet another baby might most enjoy it when you copy her sounds.

using the senses

Helping babies to look and enjoy

Developmental focus

Babies explore their world most actively with their eyes, so you need to provide activities that will stimulate their vision and are appropriate to their stage of development. From birth, babies can turn their heads towards diffuse sources of light, and react to bright light by closing their eyes. During the first weeks, babies focus best on objects 20-30cm from their eyes; the carer's face is usually at this distance when holding the baby. Toys and mobiles hanging over a cot at this distance encourage the baby to focus.

Eye-to-eye contact plays an important role in the initial stages of the development of close attachment to parents and is also important with later attachments to other key carers. By around four months, babies start to realise that when they see something they can reach out and touch it. Between six and nine months, they will look for any toy they drop. Babies at this stage particularly enjoy peek-a-boo games.

When they cannot yet move independently, babies need you to bring them interesting things to look at or to carry them to the sights to take a good look. Babies are naturally visually curious and their gaze will move over

anything of interest, being easily distracted by something else.
If you help them to look and learn in the early months, they will begin later to steadily gaze at an intriguing object. They will also use their physical skills to explore and to move the object so they can take an even better look.

The treasure basket

This idea is very flexible and promotes a broad range of learning for babies and toddlers.

Elinor Goldschmied observed the fascination babies and toddlers have with ordinary household objects and developed the idea into a learning resource that she has called the treasure basket.

- Gather a range of materials that vary in feel and texture and keep them in a low, open basket.
- Collect ordinary, safe objects like small containers, large cotton reels, fir cones, woolly balls, a firm fruit like a lemon, a wooden spoon or spatula, large wooden curtain rings, a bath sponge, a small scoop or pastry cutters and the larger type of wooden clothes peg. Avoid commercially-made toys.
- Make a collection that varies in look, texture, shape and smell so that babies can explore in any way they wish.
- Make sure that no object is small enough for a baby to swallow.
- If you use the basket with older children with learning disabilities, be aware that they may still put objects in their mouths (and their mouths will be bigger than a baby's!).

The basket is for babies who are able to sit up comfortably, either without any help or with a support for their back. Put the basket on the floor, sit one or two babies up to it and watch from close by. Let them play as they wish and do not intervene unless a baby is pushing something into his throat or hitting another baby with an item.
Give babies time to explore the objects however they want.
Toddlers often still enjoy the treasure basket and this activity can be extended into discovery or heuristic play (see page 53).

Play and learning tips

A baby's attention is caught by striking contrasts, for example soft toys like a panda or abstract patterns and paintings.

They are interested in all kinds of play materials and not just what are sold as 'baby toys'.

Follow the baby's gaze; what interests her? Be ready to repeat any games that make her smile or look intently.

Have plenty of resources to hand for the baby's visual interest, but do not overload her with too much at any one time. Let her stare, enjoy and then move on to gazing at something or someone else.

Activities

Look and learn

- Attach safe wooden and plastic utensils, strips of foil, greaseproof paper and tissues to string over a cot using bulldog clips. If they move in a slight blow of air, that will be interesting too.
- Hang a prism in the window so that spectrums appear on the wall on sunny days.
- Blow bubbles for the baby to track and perhaps reach for.
- Use bright glove puppets in tracking games. Sing 'Incy Wincy Spider' with a spider puppet.
- Play peek-a-boo games or let babies look in a mirror to see their reflections change as they move.
- Partially hide a toy under something and ask the baby to find it. Eventually, you will be able to hide the item completely when they are watching and they will be able to find it again.

A first book

- For this activity, you need empty baby milk tins (check that there are no sharp edges), photographs, magazine pictures and wrapping paper.
- Select pictures of familiar things, such as family members, animals, toys or fruit. Laminate the pictures and then glue or tape them onto the tin.
- Roll the tin for the baby to watch, pointing at and talking about the different pictures. Make comments such as 'Can you see a face?' Answer your own questions with, 'There it is.'
- As alternatives, use black-and-white squares on the tin (especially for babies up to two months). Or cover the tins with simple patterns in two colours.

Bright lights

- Make sure babies are comfortable, either sitting or lying.
- Get a torch. Dull the lights so that the beam of the torch can be seen easily. Slowly move the torch around the room.
- Watch the baby following it with their eyes. (Be careful not to flash the light in their face, as this can be distressing.)
- Extend this activity by cutting basic shapes, such as hearts or diamonds, out of different-coloured cellophane or gels and placing them over the torch. Or place a revolving lamp in the room, at a safe distance from the babies' reach.

Flying saucers

- Draw bold, simple and colourful designs on paper plates; for example, squares, giant polka-dots, stripes or stars.
- Hang the plates with ribbon around the baby in the cot or elsewhere in the nursery. Ensure they are always beyond the baby's reach when you are not there.
- As alternatives, use paper plates with pre-printed designs, or draw faces on the paper plates. Add wool for hair and make sure they are smiling!

Bring a bottle

- Collect together empty plastic bottles (individual drink size), coloured water or liquid, bubble bath, scraps of bright materials, glitter, tinsel, fabric conditioner and feathers.
- Fill the bottles with a variety of objects and coloured liquids. Then check that the bottle lids are secure.
- Shake one bottle slowly and gently in front of the baby's face. Move it from side to side, then from above the baby's head, and down again.
- Continue with the other bottles and extend this activity by using additional materials such as sequins, glass beads, shelled nuts or holographic paper.

Touch

Developmental focus

Touch is more than a physical skill; it also helps babies to learn about their own body and the world around them. Touch is also part of communication and making close contact with others. So touch plays an important role within an affectionate relationship between babies and parents or familiar carers.

In the early weeks, babies can grasp a finger placed in their hand. Between one to two months, they begin to find their own hands and experiment by holding one hand with the other and opening and shutting their fingers. By about two months, babies start to grasp a toy placed in their hands and soon learn to hold and wave the toy about. By about three months, babies can play with their hands deliberately, watching their moving fingers and putting a finger or thumb into their mouths. From three to six months, babies can learn to look at, reach out for and swipe at or grasp toys. From six to twelve months, babies are using a range of physical skills to make contact with an object, and then hold onto and explore it.

Play and learning tips

Very young babies want to feel the physical boundaries to their world. For example, when bathing young babies, hold them so that their feet touch the end of the baby bath. They will be reassured by the contact.

Talk with parents to understand how their baby likes to be touched, carried and held.

In the early months, the nerve endings in a baby's tongue, lips and mouth are more sensitive than those in their fingers. If you try to stop babies mouthing, then you deny them information about their world. Just ensure that any plaything is clean and not small enough to swallow.

Babies will use their current favourite method of touch on any object of interest. Watch them and see what they are doing each week. Do they concentrate on turning an item around or over, do they stroke or shake it, rub, drop or try to scrunch it up?

Activities

Hello there!

- Get a wakeful baby's attention with warm words and a gentle touch to his hands, cheek or body.
- Look and smile. Combine friendly conversation with physical contact, so that the baby is encouraged to communicate.
- Tune into what individual babies like. Some enjoy a gentle tickle or walking your fingers up an arm or over their stomach.
- Touch the baby's hand or stroke his cheek while murmuring friendly words.

Within reach

Help babies develop the combination of look, reach and touch.

- Place a suitable toy into the baby's hands. Talk to the baby about what you're doing. Repeat with the same or other toys for as long as the baby is interested. This may be longer than you expect!
- Provide safe mobiles that a baby can stretch out for and touch or swipe at. Watch and share in the babies' fun when their hands and the mobiles connect.
- Hold a toy steady and wait patiently for the baby to look, touch and grasp. Be pleased with him when he does, and perhaps say, 'You've got it!' Repeat with other toys that interest him.

Touch and explore

- Offer toys to squeeze and to cuddle, or soft toys or balls that make a sound when shaken.
- Have a set of simple containers and objects that can be grasped and put in and out, again and again. Try a plastic food container box and cotton reels, medium woolly balls, wooden or firm plastic spoons and some lids.
- Sit with the baby on your lap and let him touch you: your face, your hair, your collar or your jewellery. When his grasp gets stronger, gently unlock his fingers if they are hurting you.
- Babies like shiny pictures in books – to look at but also to move their fingers over. Use board books and let the baby decide when to turn the page. Make your

own shiny book with A5-size plastic envelopes and put a bright magazine or calendar picture into each one.

The human gym

- Babies need to feel with their hands and their feet and then to experience full body movement. Hold the baby with his feet firm against your lap and allow him to bounce. Show enthusiasm for the game.
- Lie on the floor and let the baby crawl over you. Or sit and let him lean against your back. Play crawling-chasing on a soft floor. (Don't stop at twelve months; toddlers love these games too!)

Learning and making contact through smell

Developmental focus

Smell is probably the most underrated sense and, like touch, is far more than just a physical sense. When a baby enters the world, smell is perhaps more important to her than at any other point in her life. The sense of smell plays an important role in the bonding process between babies and their carers. Within a week, babies can distinguish their own mother's and another mother's milk on breast pads placed near their noses. Even within the early weeks, babies will turn their heads away from smells that they appear to find unpleasant.

Babies have limited clear vision beyond their focussing point and need to make sense of what they are experiencing. So, new-born babies may rely on smell to give them a better understanding of the world, of what is familiar and unfamiliar. Through their sense of smell they can gather information about where they are and who the person close by or holding them is. A baby will be aware of different smells as you take her from one area to another, both inside and outside.

Play and learning tips

Before doing any smell activities with babies (or older under threes) do check with parents to see if the children have any allergies. Be prepared to have this conversation again later, since some allergies and sensitivities take time to emerge. Keep a record of each child's allergies with their other personal records.

If there is any concern that a baby or young child might be allergic to something in the activity, then place the perfumes, petals, and so on, on small sticky-backed address labels, which can then be worn on their clothing, to avoid direct contact with their hands, eyes or noses. If babies or children in the group are known to be severely allergic to anything, avoid activities that include those allergens.

Familiar smells can be emotionally significant to a baby or young child. For instance, never wash a baby or child's comfort blanket or special toy without checking with the parents first. Unless they say it is safe to wash the item and the child will not be distressed, just sponge off any spillages.

As well as special activities with smells, be alert to everyday smells, such as warm milk or food. Show the baby you are enjoying the aroma and say something like, 'mashed apple, my favourite!'

Activities

Fun with smells

- Make a smelly frieze. These can be just as interesting as the tactile friezes that nurseries often make for babies to explore.
- Burn different oils and essences in a burner each week.
- Hang oranges with cloves around the playroom.
- Make mobiles for cots or changing mats using pot pourri or herbs.

Bags of perfume

- Sprinkle fresh herbs and spices on to individual nappy liners, wrap them with different, brightly-coloured pieces of tulle and tie them with a length of ribbon.
- Dangle the bags one at a time in front of the baby. Encourage the baby to reach out and draw the scented bag towards her face.
- Let the baby play with the bag and experience the smell.
- Alternatively, put wooden scented fruits or flower petals inside the bags.

Book of smells

- Make a small book by soaking cotton swatches or dry nappy liners in scent, for example, pine needles, shampoo, lavender or rose, and allow to dry.
- Then cut a shape related to the scent, for example a flower or a tree, in the centre of an A4-size piece of card.
- Glue the smelly cotton material on to a full page then place and glue the cut-out over the top. The scented material should be seen through the cut-out shape.
- 'Read' the book with the baby, telling her about the cut-out shape, the colour, and so on. Offer the page to the baby to smell.
- Repeat the appropriate words as the baby experiences the page. This is warm conversation as part of the activity; you are not expecting the baby to learn the words.
- Add new pages each day but let the baby enjoy the old favourites as well.

Smelly socks

- For this activity, you will need brightly-coloured baby socks, cotton balls, a length of elastic and pleasant spices such as cloves or cinnamon.
- Shake a pleasant-smelling spice on to the cotton balls and put them inside a sock.
- Tie the top of the sock and sew elastic on to the top, hanging it above the changing table or cot.
- Pull the sock and offer it to the baby or toddler. Once they have experienced the smell, let the sock bounce.
- Encourage the child to pull the sock towards her nose to smell it.
- To extend this activity put fruit, vegetables or pot pourri into the socks. Decorate the socks by drawing faces on

them or sewing some bells around the top.

Scented tissues

- You will need a box of 15 to 20 citrus-scented tissues.
- Give the box to the toddler and let her pull out the tissues.
- Take tissues that have been pulled out of the box and show the child how to roll them into balls, encouraging her to copy.
- Play silly games with the tissue balls. Put one on your head and let it fall off. Let her try the same.
- Put as many as you can in your hand and scrunch them, say 'Abracadabra' and open your hand so the balls can fall out.

Listening to and enjoying sound

Developmental focus

Babies have a well-developed sense of hearing from birth – they have to make sense of what they hear from voices and the sounds of everyday life.

A baby will have heard many different sounds in the womb, including her mother's heartbeat and rumbling stomach. It is important for parents to talk even with tiny babies, because the sound of the parents' voices helps in the bonding process. It also builds on the baby's acute sense of smell. Because babies focus on high-pitched sounds, they tend to smile and laugh when adults raise the pitch of their voices, which also encourages the adult to continue interacting in this way. This pattern of talking with babies is called infant-directed speech (see also page 26). Babies need to be able to focus on sounds and to distinguish slowly the meaning of everyday routine sounds. Such experience is crucial to ensure that hearing becomes a key sense in supporting their ability to concentrate later in early childhood.

Play and learning tips

Babies will be startled by loud sounds, so the gentle, quiet approach is more appropriate to younger ones.

Be alert to what each individual baby likes. Some babies like quiet, soothing sounds, some may like their sounds a bit noisier.

Avoid having undifferentiated background sounds (for instance, from a radio) even if it is not very loud. It becomes unhelpful sound 'wallpaper'.

A continuous sound encourages the baby to turn her eyes towards the noise, and shaking a rattle or repeating her name will generally develop her hearing. Never persist with a sound game that seems to make the baby uneasy or jumpy.

Singing gently or reciting rhymes are ideal ways to calm a distressed baby. Share rhymes with parents by telling them the songs you sing and learning some of theirs.

You can buy commercially-produced sensory toys for babies that include sounds. However, you will give baby more variety if you make your own.

Activities

Listen and look

- Play different kinds of background music at various times of the day.
- Hang rustling kites, mobiles or wind chimes from the ceiling.
- Play peek-a-boo games accompanied by friendly noises.
- Involve the babies in lots of singing, interacting with them by using your facial expressions and tickling them.
- Create noise-makers from plastic bottles filled with pasta, lentils, coloured pasta shapes, bells, rice, beads or sequins. Make sure the lid is fixed firmly.

Noisy boards

- Collect three or four thick pieces of cardboard or plywood squares (30cm x 30cm), bright sheets of cellophane, coloured plastic bags, silver foil and strips of crinkly material and four colours of paint.
- Paint the boards in bright colours, making sure they have no sharp edges. Glue the ends of the strips of cellophane, foil, material and bags firmly on each of the boards.
- While the baby is sitting in her chair, offer each board separately to her. Rustle the materials gently – then more vigorously.
- Encourage the baby to rustle the materials by first putting them within reach of her hands, then perhaps within reach of her toes.
- If the baby is content, place her on the floor beside, or surrounded by, the boards. Let her experiment and make sounds with the materials, under close supervision.

Whisper, whisper

- Sit the baby on your knee. Chat to her in soft tones, then louder tones – low and then higher voices.
- Make faces at the baby while repeating her name and 'Hello'. Repeat her name to either side of her, behind and in front, quietly then in different tones and pitches.
- Kiss the baby on both cheeks, repeating the word 'kiss' in different tones and pitches. Cuddle the baby while repeating the word 'cuddle', 'tickle' and so on.
- Sit the baby in a suitable baby chair or baby nest and whisper a variety of words while holding up a visual aid, such as a teddy, duck or rattle. Use different accents, or sing-song rhythm when saying the words.

Noisy mobiles

- Collect a wooden or padded coat hanger, bells, string, foil, milk bottle tops, rattle, cellophane, sweet wrappers, beads, brightly-coloured thin ribbons and one large wooden curtain ring.
- Attach the items tightly to the coat hanger with the ribbons. Ensure that one ribbon is much longer than the others and

attach the curtain ring to the end of the longer ribbon.

■ Hang the mobile above the baby's cot or changing station so she can reach the curtain ring and use this as a handle to shake the other items.

■ Talk to the baby about what is going on and the interesting sounds being made.

Musical gloves

■ Sew small bells to a brightly- coloured pair of gloves, one on each glove.

■ Give the baby one glove at a time and urge her to shake her hand. Then give her both gloves.

■ If she is enjoying this game, tie brightly-coloured ribbons with small bells to the baby's wrists. Take them off as soon as the game is complete.

Instant percussion

■ Make a collection of plastic containers, wooden boxes, saucepans, biscuit tins, wooden and metal spoons, plastic egg cups and a sieve.

■ Sit the baby on the floor and place a variety of containers within her reach. Offer her a spoon and allow her to beat the various containers.

■ Join in, talking about the noises and sounds being created.

■ Lift two of the egg cups and bang them gently together. Offer them to the baby and allow her to experiment.

■ Use a spoon to run round and over the surface of the containers rather than beating. Offer a spoon to the baby and again allow her to play.

■ Let her explore real instruments such as drums, castanets and maracas.

When to worry

Some babies will have disabilities related to the senses. It is far from easy to recognise and assess visual or hearing loss in very young babies. However, parents and other key carers are usually the first to be uneasy that something is amiss.

■ Use your observation skills to be alert to babies who do not appear to react to sounds or do not gaze in the way that is usual.

■ Babies usually respond to the stimulation of all the senses, although they will be less responsive of course if they are tired, hungry or unwell.

■ Share your concerns, with care, with a parent and listen if they have worries. The parent may welcome your support in seeking an expert opinion if you are both concerned.

■ You also need to share any concerns about sensitivities or allergies that become clear through everyday care routines.

language and creative development

Early Communication

Developmental focus

Babies communicate from their earliest weeks, many months before their first recognisable words. Their crying becomes more varied and they make sounds that reflect their mood. A baby's increasing control of his mouth, tongue and lips means that he will become able to make an ever wider range of sounds. By five to six months babies are making strings of sounds. They smile and chuckle to engage your attention – or just for sheer pleasure.

Between about six and twelve months, babies become adept at communicating with a range of vocalisations through sound-making. They also use the full support of their facial expressions and useful gestures like pointing, to direct your attention and share their current interests. Babies need to be able to hear clear words, in a meaningful context, before they will start to understand and use words spontaneously.

Play and learning tips

You are the very best item of play equipment to help babies learn to communicate. They need caring adults to respond with interest and enthusiasm to all their early efforts.

Get into the habit of baby-watching: how does this individual baby make sounds, what gestures does she make?

Babies and young children have to be able to hear you, to distinguish sounds, and then words, easily. So cut down on unnecessary background noise and avoid bad habits like raising your voice regularly or shouting.

Have quiet, as well as lively times, and help babies to tell the difference.

Be physically close; neither you nor the baby can communicate from a distance. Babies need to be sure that you are talking with or listening to them.

Take your time with individual babies. Don't rush from one baby to another; they will get confused.

Activities

Mutual gazing

- Very young babies stare at you, often in a very concentrated way.
- Hold the baby in your arms, look back and smile.
- Say simple words in a soft and friendly tone. It does not matter what you say, perhaps, 'Hello, how are you doing this lovely morning?' or 'Shall we walk about a bit then? Would you like that?'
- Older babies still enjoy a peaceful gaze, with a grin and touch.

First 'conversations'

- From around two months babies enjoy and learn from simple exchanges.
- Say something, then pause for the baby to reply with sounds or waving arms and legs.
- Then it is your turn again to say some words, to smile and make friendly sounds or facial expressions.
- Keep looking at the baby and sometimes copy her lead, perhaps she makes a cooing sound or gives a broad grin. Babies are thrilled when you repeat their sound or expression back to them.

Let's have a chat

- It does not matter what you say to babies so long as you sound interesting. Research suggests that it does matter how you talk with babies. Babies react best to what is now called infant-directed speech.
- The trick is to talk in a more expressive way than you might to older children or adults. Repeat yourself in slightly different words. Talk more slowly than usual and leave pauses for the baby to join the 'conversation'.
- For instance, you might say with a light tone throughout, 'I had a terrible time on the bus this morning (pause and look at the baby). Oh, yes I did (pause and a smile). That bus would not come (pause). No it wouldn't (pause) and I got so cold waiting (pause). You're grinning, yes you are (pause and a smile). You don't mind me getting cold (pause). What a one you are (pause and affectionate touch). You just wait until you have to go on the bus, yes, you just wait'... and so on in a circling way that engages the baby's interest.
- Talk simply about what you are doing in the baby's physical care routines.
- Use simple language such as, 'Let's take your hat off', or, 'Here's your drink'.

Add the words

- Listen, watch and respond to the baby's sounds, expressions and gestures. Add some words that are appropriate to the situation.
- If he stretches out a hand towards the teddy, you say, 'Do you want the teddy?' as you hand it over.
- If his eyes swivel round at the sound of someone entering the room, say, 'Look, it's Marsha. Shall we say "Hello" to Marsha?'

Ooh look!

- Within the second half of the first year, babies start to point: a very useful social skill to engage your attention and share their interests and wishes.
- Show babies that you are interested in

what catches their attention.

- Add your simple comments about what the baby can directly experience through his senses.
- Follow his excited point with, 'Oh, yes, look. It's our robin back again'. Show delight in the tinkling made by his rattle with, 'Listen, you made it work. Can I have a go?'
- Respond to what the baby notices close by with comments like, 'Yes, Jamal's crying, isn't he', or, 'That's right, there's our lunch coming in. Are you hungry? I am.'

Peek-a-boo

- Babies are intrigued by people or toys who temporarily disappear.
- Play peek-a-boo by moving in and out of the baby's vision. Say, 'Hello!' as you reappear.
- Cover your head with a cloth that you or the baby pulls off.
- If the baby wants, let her cover her head. Say, 'Where's Sally? Where's she gone?' and then, 'There you are!'. (Toddlers still love this game as well and may like you to cover their whole body.)

Is it a game?

- Follow the baby's lead when something she enjoys doing can turn into a game shared with you.
- It might be making a funny face with the lips puckered up, blowing raspberries, pointing and chuckling or putting her hand on the page of a book so you cannot turn it over.
- Add suitable words to the game, such as, 'What a face that is!' or 'Can't I turn the page then? No?'
- If you do not want something to turn into a game, like the baby spraying out food, then do your level best not to laugh, even if it is funny the first time.
- Babies like games when you or the baby gives something and takes it back, perhaps many times. Add words like, 'Is this for me?' and 'Oh, you want it back. I thought it was mine', accompanied by smiles.
- Babies like to throw or drop something and have you fetch and give it back, often to the accompaniment of smiles and chortles from the baby.

Babies make their mark

Developmental focus

As they make early attempts to manipulate materials themselves, Babies are naturally drawn to artistic and creative materials which stimulate all their senses.

It is important to allow very young children to learn how to manipulate and use a wide range of materials at their own pace. They are discovering their world in terms of 'What is this?' and 'What can I do with that?'. Babies will learn best if allowed to explore: holding, looking at and banging things together. They will not learn if pushed to handle materials in the one 'right' way or to produce a particular response that pleases adults.

Babies are learning about creative materials long before they have

reached the developmental stage when they can manipulate and use materials to produce recognisable marks or shapes. They enjoy opportunities to explore and experiment with colour, shape, texture and pattern. Babies learn about these qualities by hands-on experience for months before it is appropriate to see if they are ready for the words that label the ideas.

Play and learning tips

All these activities should be undertaken in an informal and subtle manner, following the pace of the baby's interests. Relax with the baby, take your time and she will enjoy and learn.

Babies are absorbed in the processes involved in using creative materials and relish using all their senses.

Babies love to explore, so create activities that allow them to experiment with a range of resources. Resist any temptation to operate a 'conveyor belt' pushing babies to make hand or fruit prints. What on earth would the babies gain from this?

If your sense of pressure comes from parents who want evidence of 'what my baby did today', then take photos of fun early art activities and make copies for parents. Talk about what you all did and invite parents to come and join you.

All the following activities need your attentive and close involvement for safety. Some of the materials could cause harm if used inappropriately – but will be safe if you are there.

Activities

Artistic appreciation

■ Hang objects with different patterns, shapes and colours on the walls at an appropriate level.

■ On the baby gym, dangle brightly-coloured ribbons, beads and bells. Encourage the baby to reach up to shake, push or pull.

■ Share books that have interesting patterns, textures, colours and shapes with babies.

Art gallery

■ Carry babies to look closely at pictures or posters on your wall. They often like to stare at 'real art'. Make a few comments such as 'I like that'.

- Interest babies with simple pictures, shapes and patterns. Laminate these and tie them securely in the baby's cot, changing the pictures regularly.
- Young babies especially like simple pictures with contrasting colours or black-and-white patterns.

Sensory art

- Offering a baby 3-D shapes to play with will allow him to explore and experience shape.
- Create a treasure basket with basic shapes – a ball, a marble egg, a cylinder of wood, a square toy brick, a prism or an apple.
- Allow the baby to explore different textures by making a mural he can touch. Include satin, silk, wool, cotton, corduroy, velvet, sandpaper, tissue paper, wallpaper and so on.
- Put yoghurt, whipping cream, instant whip and beans on to a baby's high chair tray. Let the baby feel the texture and experiment with the patterns they can make.
- Make different coloured jellies. Place blobs of jelly on a piece of paper and let the baby mix them together. Don't worry if he eats it.
- Give babies experience of different coloured themes. When using green, you could put a dark green towel over her bouncy chair and hang a variety of green pieces of material, ribbons or cellophane over his play mat. A set of bottles with green marbles, green bubble bath, green tissue balls and green tinsel can be offered to the baby to grasp and shake. (Be very clear for yourself and for parents, that you are offering visual experience of colour and, not in any sense, getting babies to know their colours.)

My first picture

- Mix a little washable paint and water with cereal, for example Weetabix.
- Place this on the baby's high chair tray. Stay close so the baby doesn't eat it and let him create a design with the mixture.
- Place a sheet of paper over the design to take a print of it if you want to have a 'first picture'.

Musical babies

Developmental focus

Research shows that a musically-enriched home environment has an influence on the development of a child's musical ability. Not every child will want to play a musical instrument later in childhood, but they can all enjoy and make music.

The more opportunities children are given to explore and practise particular skills, the more confident they will become in using them in different situations. Babies experiment with making sounds that are pleasing to them. Adults can build on this development by encouraging babies to interact with them when singing lullabies and rhymes.

Babies will be startled by loud sounds, so a gentle, quiet approach is most appropriate. As their ability to manipulate objects develops, babies become interested in particular objects with which they can make sounds. They relish their ability to make something happen, in this case a noise of some kind.

Play and learning tips

Calm restless babies by singing or playing gentle, quiet songs to them whilst swaying them gently.

When changing, feeding, dressing and bathing babies, say rhymes or sing songs to them.

Babies like and start to recognise songs and rhymes that are short and contain lots of repetition. Extend your knowledge of songs and rhymes and build in new ones that you learn from families of a different cultural background to yourself.

Babies like a wide range of songs and music, not just those designed exclusively for very young children.

Vary the tone of your voice when talking to babies. They like hearing sounds that change – monotones are boring to them.

Activities

Making music

- Hang up a set of wind chimes.
- Hang music boxes from the mobiles in your nursery.
- Build a collection of old sets of keys to shake for attention.
- Use songs that lend themselves to playing with fingers and toes, for example, 'This Little Piggy...'.
- Tie bells securely to the baby's gloves or booties to encourage him to make a sound by shaking his hands or feet. Take the gloves off when the game is over.
- Occasionally play music for babies to listen to and enjoy.

Songs to make friends by

This activity helps the development of a warm attachment between you and the babies in your care, so they can feel more secure in the nursery.

- Hold the baby securely and whilst gently swaying him, smile and look into his eyes.
- Sing a variety of songs such as, 'Peek-a-boo' and 'Pat-a-cake'.
- Make sure you use songs with different tempos, sung in different voices. Change the baby's position while singing.
- Make the songs interactive by touching parts of the baby's body as you sing.

Shake it

- Wash out four litre-sized juice cartons. Cover them with wrapping paper, holographic paper, coloured foil and other eye-catching coverings.
- Place small bells inside two of the cartons. Leave the other two empty, and secure all the containers.
- Let the babies shake the cartons. Respond with a facial gesture or surprised noise when they shake the ones with bells inside.

Playing the spoons

■ Give the baby a wooden spoon. Allow him to bang it on different surfaces: on thick paper, a table top, tin foil, cellophane and on a woolly jumper.
■ Give the baby a large metal spoon and encourage the same experiment again.
■ Give the baby a metal pan to bang on using either of the spoons.

Hide-and-seek

■ This activity can be done inside or outdoors on a grassy area
■ Get a musical toy or box. Wind it up and hide it.
■ Ask the baby, 'What's that noise – where's it coming from?'
■ Start looking for it by crawling around together. Congratulate the baby when you find it.
■ Hide it in the same place a few times to build up confidence, then eventually change the location where it is hidden.

Music and movement

■ Play a variety of music. Hold the baby and dance to the music.
■ Play fast and slow music, loud and soft music, pieces with high and low sounds. See what individual babies like the most.
■ Bounce the baby on your lap in time to the music. Change the baby's position as you listen, holding him over one shoulder, then the other.
■ Show the baby different ways to move to music: clap, march or sway back and forth when sitting.
■ If babies are secure to stand up by holding onto a low table, see if they want to bounce to the music while supporting themselves.

Musical mats

■ Gather about ten coloured face cloths. Glue or sew a variety of objects onto them, such as bells, buttons, scrunched-up silver foil, cotton wool and bubble wrap.
■ Sew all the face cloths together or leave as individual mats.
■ Sit the babies beside the mat or surround them with the smaller ones.
■ Give them a large spoon and allow them to use the spoon or their hand to make a sound. Show them how to make sounds if necessary.
■ Adapt this activity by placing a bed sheet or large sheet of thick paper on the floor or grass. On one area put sand or salt, on another cotton wool and on a third silver foil. Let the baby move about exploring sounds they can make.

Copy cat

■ Take photos of babies making 'music' – clapping, banging a container, hitting two spoons or shaking some bells.
■ Put the photos in a small album or photo cube.
■ Show the baby one photo at a time and talk about it. Show the photo again and offer the 'instrument' to play.
■ Don't expect babies to recognise themselves; and you are not of course expecting them to learn the names of the home-made instruments.

Stories for babies

Developmental focus

Babies enjoy stories because this activity combines closeness to a key carer, recognisable sounds and the visual images of suitable books. Telling a story or looking at books with babies is a time of emotional and physical closeness. A baby feels the warmth of attention from the adult through this shared activity and when you return to the baby's favourite books or oral stories, you support her emotional development.

Good stories, story-songs and story-rhymes for babies unfold with a recognisable rhythm, that even under ones start to recognise with a big grin and perhaps waving of arms in pleasure. This experience helps babies to tune into sounds and sound patterns as they occur in everyday speech. This phonemic awareness, enjoyed without pressure from the early months, lays the foundations for language and, much later, for literacy.

Play and learning tips

Continue to build your resources of good books for babies, stories, story-songs and story-rhymes. Ask parents for ideas and draw on the different cultural groups represented in your setting, as well as looking a little further afield.

Share all kinds of stories when babies are interested. Don't restrict yourself to a scheduled story time, be flexible to the moment and then babies will be interested and learn.

You absolutely do not have to be a good singer or performer. Babies are not music or theatre critics! Just be expressive in how you sing or say the rhyme. Enjoy yourself and the baby will too.

Activities

Listen to the rhythm

- Even very young babies enjoy a story told through song, rhyme and gentle touch. They start to tune into the sound and rhythm of your voice long before they recognise the individual words.
- Try out different song stories with babies, such as 'Pat-a-cake', 'This little piggy' or 'See-saw Marjorie Daw'.
- Be alert to individual favourites. A smile or happy sound will tell you that even a three-month-old baby now recognises and likes a particular song. Share this learning with parents.
- Extend your range of more conventional lullabies and rhymes for babies. However, many babies like 'grown up' story songs, such as old music hall favourites like 'Daisy, Daisy'.

Stories with movement

- Create some simple hand movements or gentle touch to fit a baby's favourite song or rhyme and keep to the same pattern whenever you tell this story. The baby will start to anticipate the gestures, soft tickles or being bounced on your lap or along your stretched out legs.

■ By the time babies are about six months, try a definite pause before the final line of a story song, or the hand movement accompanying a rhyme. See if the baby looks expectant and then enjoy the final words or gesture with him.

Books for babies

■ You need to be close to babies when you tell a story in any format. They should be on your lap or you can be sitting together on a comfortable floor or big cushion. You will face a baby when you tell a story through song or rhyme but make sure that you are alongside with a book, both looking at it from the same angle.

■ Tell the story at the child's pace. Sometimes she will want more time to stare at the picture in a book, touch the illustrations and feel any special parts of the book that are designed for touching as well as looking.

■ Select a few suitable books to share together but be ready to follow the baby's own choice as soon as she shows a preference.

■ Leave the stronger board books easily available for babies, so that they can choose and look at them whenever they want. Books with paper pages can be kept in a box or file and brought out when you can show how to handle them gently.

physical development

Getting on the move

Developmental focus

Within the first year of life babies will become mobile, if all goes well. Watch them and see how hard they work at it. Their perseverance is amazing.

A baby gradually develops the ability to control whole body movements. These movements are often referred to as gross motor skills. During the time in the womb, a baby has already been practising physical movements, although in an increasingly confined area in the final months. New-borns have limited voluntary control over their bodies and limbs and the physical control moves from the head steadily down their bodies.

At around one month, a baby may start to wave his arms and legs, kicking and splashing in the bath. At around three months, the baby's back gets firmer and he may start to lift up his head and chest when lying on his stomach, using the elbows, forearms and hands as support. He may start to move arms and legs more smoothly and start reaching towards objects. By six months, babies may roll over from front to back and raise their arms to show they want to be picked up. They may sit unaided for short periods. By about nine months, many babies will be on the move. They may try to wriggle along on their stomachs or crawl along on the floor. Some may bottom-shuffle in a sitting position, using their legs to propel them forward. By twelve months, many babies can get into the sitting position from lying down. They may walk around holding furniture or an adult's hand for support. Some will be walking without help.

Play and learning tips

Young babies need all the necessary support for their bodies that they cannot yet provide themselves. In the early weeks, this means safe support for their relatively heavy heads.

Watch them as over the weeks and months, their physical control moves down their bodies. Notice how persistently they work at this challenging task.

Babies have a very strong drive to use their bodies and to practise all their skills. They need safe space for moving around, and often the best area will be on a comfortable floor.

Don't be in a rush to get babies or toddlers to sit up to a table for activities. Be prepared to play on the floor with them, enjoying the play materials or letting them crawl all over you.

Mobile babies want and need to practise their skills and become more confident through a fair amount of repetition. Provide them with safe spaces and admire what they manage.

Activities

Baby exercises!

- Create a padded area with lots of floor space where the babies can move around.
- Encourage use of baby gyms so they can stretch up, swing their arms and kick their legs.
- Dangle something over baby's feet to encourage kicking.
- Let babies move freely on a variety of textures – a pile carpet, linoleum, or fresh, clean grass. Get down and join babies as they creep, crawl or shuffle.

Baby reach

- Hold a variety of objects above the baby's head to encourage stretching.
- Play with toys beyond the baby's grasp. This will encourage the baby to stretch and explore the items when they retrieve them.
- Move around to encourage the baby to move after you.
- Treasure baskets develop large muscles when stretching for items in the basket, waving and shaking them. They also give babies practice in sitting unaided, or with safe back support, when they are ready.

Stretch and grow!

- Remove the baby's clothes and lay him on a soft quilt or mat.
- Play gentle, pleasant background music that you can keep time to. Or develop a song that goes with the following exercises; the baby will soon recognise the opening words and notes of your special song.
- Place the baby on his back and let him grasp your thumbs. Raise his right arm over his head, then his left.
- Place the baby on his back and clasp his legs in your hands. Hold them straight, then bend them gently towards his chest, and repeat the sequence.

Cushion games

- Put cushions, bean bags and pillows in a pile on the floor.
- Allow the baby to explore the mountain of scattered cushions.
- Pick up a cushion or roll over it and the baby may copy you.
- Hide behind the cushions and play some 'peek-a-boo' games.

Bouncing rhymes

- Sit the baby on your lap facing you. Hold the baby under his arms and move forward until you are sitting on the edge of the chair.
- Lift your heels so the baby gets a good bounce while you recite some bouncing rhymes, such as, 'Horsy, horsy' or 'Yankee doodle'.
- Sit on the chair with your knees crossed. Rest the baby over your foot and grasp his hands firmly. Lift your leg up and down. Keep your foot close to the floor and the baby will eventually push his feet off the floor in response.

Flying games

- Try these games when the baby can hold his head up on his own.
- Lie on the floor and gently lift the baby up and down.
- Holding your hands under the baby's armpits or around his chest, move the baby backwards and forwards and from side to side.
- Move the baby in all directions. Slowly and gently dip the baby's head, and then feet, towards you.
- If the baby likes this game add some bounces, lifts and wiggles. Talk or sing to the baby.

Rolling bottles

- Use your collection of filled plastic bottles (activity on page 18) and place them on a large carpeted area where the baby can stretch, touch and explore them freely.

Seeing, reaching and grasping

Developmental focus

As well as the larger physical movements, babies are developing their finer control, in combination with vision and touch. Fine motor activities and skills are those that involve small muscle movements in the hands, feet and mouth, often in co-ordination with the eyes. A baby gradually develops the ability to concentrate and control these movements, but first has to realise that her body parts belong to her.

Any activity that stimulates the hands will help babies realise they are in control of them. They start to play with their fingers, while focusing their eyes on them, from around three months. During the second half of the first year, babies experiment with different ways of exploring materials through physical manipulation, and they tend to use their favourite method on anything. Babies explore through holding, squeezing, throwing and dropping, rubbing and scrunching, turning over and around or poking. They do not know enough about the world to keep themselves safe, nor to distinguish play materials from valuable adult possessions, so that is your job. By their first birthday, most babies will reach out to grasp objects and put them in their mouths. They start to manipulate objects with increasing control using the pincer grasp – the co-ordination of the index finger and thumb.

Play and learning tips

Provide a wide variety of items that babies can hold, shake, lift, push and pull. As they tend to put things in their mouths, make sure that play materials are too large to be swallowed and are also washable.

Have a broad choice of everyday objects and not just commercially-made 'official' baby toys. Babies can be interested in anything.

All the following activities require close supervision. They are only suitable for play with babies when you are continuously involved. It is not at all safe to give the babies any of these materials and then to leave them, even if it seems like a very short time to you. During these activities, you are an essential playmate.

Activities

Grab, push and pull

- Hang mobiles so that the baby can reach towards them and stroke the baby's palms to encourage clasping. When the baby has clasped an object in one hand, pass him another object to encourage use of both hands.
- Activity centres and mats may encourage babies to push, pull, dial, prod, screw and hit.
- You could also let them play with old telephones, either with dials or touch pads.
- Place some set jelly in a plastic bag or rubber glove and tie it securely. Let the baby experiment with it.

- A treasure basket (see page 16) encourages babies to develop their fine motor skills as they explore and play with the different objects. Stimulate their five senses by providing a variety of textures, shapes, weights, scents, colours, forms and lengths. Offer items that the babies can scrunch, bang, ring, tinkle or scrape.

Pull the scarf

- Hang a colourful silk scarf loosely around your neck and dangle the end of it in front of the baby.
- Encourage the baby to grab and pull your scarf off.
- Throw scarves or tissues into the air, for the baby to reach out and grab.

Washing line

- Tie a length of string at a very low level in the nursery. Drape different types of material, in strips, over the string.
- Encourage the babies to reach towards the strips of material and pull them off.

■ Stay close all the time and take the line down as soon as the game is complete.

Which hand?

■ Place the baby's favourite toy in one of your hands. Put both of your hands behind your back.

■ Encourage the baby to point to which hand they think it's in, praising and encouraging him.

Fill it up!

■ Place the baby in a comfortable position and give her a safe container.

■ Scatter rollers, clothes pegs, crayons or fir cones around the baby and, as you play, encourage the baby to pick up objects and place them inside the container. Drop a few from a small height to make a satisfying sound.

■ As an alternative, use foodstuffs such as cubes of bread or pieces of cereal. Stay close and encourage the baby to place them in a plastic carton.

Pasta play

■ Place a large bowl of cool, cooked pasta on the floor and sit one or two babies on either side of it.

■ Allow them to explore the pasta and lift it into other, smaller bowls and then back, while enjoying the slippery texture.

Face work out

■ Sit the baby opposite you. Smile, frown, make a sad face, look surprised, and see if the baby joins in.

■ Make noises to go with the expressions.

■ Follow any funny faces that the baby makes. Follow her lead.

■ Do the same activity with a mirror if the baby wants.

using the environment

Getting outside

Developmental focus

Babies are ready to be interested in almost anything - and there are rich sources of learning outside as well as indoors. By two to three months, babies are well able to focus beyond their close visual field and to be intrigued by sights at a slight distance. Over the following months, their head and body control steadily enables them to turn to what catches their attention and to reach out and touch objects.

In the second half of their first year, babies' increased mobility means that you have to watch them carefully in the garden, as anywhere else. However, since you will be there enjoying the outdoors with the babies, this is not a problem. Babies will benefit from getting out in the air. Wrap them as warmly as they need for the day's weather.

Play and learning tips

Get out with the babies and enjoy the outdoors. You will benefit as well as them.

If babies take a nap out of doors in fine weather, sit out with them. Don't view a garden as somewhere you put babies and leave them. Certainly don't put them to sleep outside in cool or cold weather. If you would not want to sit out there, don't put the babies out!

Activities

Sight and sound

- Find a sheltered place in your garden that still means babies can watch what is going on and lay out a thick rug or other ground covering for you all.
- Try to see the garden from the babies' viewpoint. Lie on your stomach alongside the babies who can lift their heads to look around. Sit with them or hold babies on your lap as they sit or stretch up on their legs supported, to look forward or

over your shoulder at what is happening behind you.

- Watch and listen with the babies, enjoying what intrigues them. Ask them, 'What can you see then?' and 'Is it the birds?'
- Enjoy the sight and sound of swooping and chattering sparrows, coloured blossoms, petals falling to the ground or the trees swaying.
- Add some visual and sound points of interest to your garden such as wind chimes and other sound-making mobiles, flags or streamers that will catch in the breeze.

Watching the world go by

- If you have a front yard or step, sit out with the babies and wave to passers-by or watch the neighbourhood cats.
- If the entrance to your nursery is on too busy a road, then try watching from a window.
- Comment simply on what you both see and express your enjoyment as well. Sometimes follow the baby's gaze and other times call her attention to something interesting with, 'Ooh, look!'

What's that?

- Walk the baby about the garden, stopping to show them flowers or the nursery rabbit. Drop some petals or leaves for the baby to watch float to the ground.
- Select some items of interest that they can touch, like soft leaves or a flower. Make sure plants are not pulled into the baby's mouth and wipe their hands afterwards.
- Towards the end of the first year, babies who cannot yet walk alone like to be hand-walked around the garden. Go at their chosen pace, looking, listening, smelling, touching and commenting.

Tumble play

- On a warm enough day, take some of the babies' books and play materials out onto the rug and enjoy their usual play in the fresh air.
- Enjoy physical play on the rug. Try some gentle body wrestling with the babies, or let them crawl over you as you lie flat out and under the tunnel you make when on your hands and knees.

Splashing about

Developmental focus

Babies enjoy sensory experiences and water offers rich material for their learning. Babies usually like the feel of warm water on their hands, feet and bodies. They enjoy their growing physical abilities to touch, splash and move water around. Even young babies can make things happen with water as the main material. Water is a feature of babies' physical care routines and can be a source of playful interest to them.

Play and learning tips

Babies must be watched carefully when they are close to water, even if it is only a few centimetres in depth. Your responsibility is always to be very close at hand.

Check the temperature of the water. Keep it warm for babies – not too hot but not cold either.

Check with parents that their babies are neither allergic nor sensitive to bubble mixes before you add these to water play. Talk again with parents because some allergies appear later in childhood.

Ensure that any play materials used are not so small as to be a risk to babies.

Activities

Water care

- Babies experience water through being washed and changed. A gentle wiping of the face or hands can be a pleasant stroking experience and shows care for the child (in contrast, for instance, with some adults' childhood memories of rough wiping with a damp, cold flannel!).
- If you are responsible for bathing babies in your work, then hold them securely, letting their feet touch the end of the baby bath. Trickle warm water over their bodies and make the cleaning process as gentle as possible. Talk with the baby as you bathe him.
- As babies' legs and arms become stronger, enjoy the play with them as they manage to splash and stir the water about.
- Let them try to catch hold of bath toys as they bob on the water. Show enthusiasm with, 'You nearly got it!' or 'Go on, try again!'

Water play

- When setting up water play, prepare to get wet. Have a warm, dry towel at the ready.
- Sit with the baby on your lap and a shallow container of warm water on a low table. Alternatively, you can sit on the floor with the baby – whatever will be safer and more comfortable in your setting.
- Let the baby watch and push about some floating bath toys. Push a toy under the water a little and then let it bounce back up.
- Let a sponge soak up the water and then squeeze it out from a short height. Show your appreciation of the stream of water with 'Ooh, look.'
- Make little waves and mini-whirlpools with your hand so that boats or ducks bob and swirl.
- Pour some water from a small plastic jug or toy watering can. Let the baby watch and put a hand or fingers into the flow as it splashes into the bowl.
- Hold an empty plastic bottle under the water and create bubbles as the water drives out the air. Empty the container from a suitable height and, if the baby looks interested, do it again.
- Use appropriate baby bath mix to make

some bubbles that the baby will try to touch and catch.

■ Provide very small amounts of water on the baby's highchair tray or a table top to be hit, splashed and pushed about a little. This game may be part of your wiping up after meal times.

Outdoor water play

■ Take advantage of warm weather and let older babies paddle their feet or sit in a safe paddling pool in the garden.
Stay very close and watch them all the time; do not turn your back even for a few seconds.

■ Babies enjoy the sense of having few, if any, clothes on and splashing the water vigorously. Give them some plastic cups or other containers to play with. Pour some water over their arms and legs.

■ Visits to a commercial paddling pool or suitable swimming pool for very young children are more likely to be possible if you work as a nanny; although some nurseries may be able to organise trips with parents' support.

■ In this larger expanse of water, go at the babies' pace. Some babies and toddlers are wary of pools. Some may think this is a huge plot to wash their hair, an activity some young children heartily dislike. So, do not go further into the water than they want and only splash the water as much as they enjoy. Leisure pools with a very gentle slope are ideal, since babies can sit with you at the edge or lean against you.

Views on the big wide world

Developmental focus

Within the first couple of months, the visual field of babies remains relatively close to them – but soon their interest is caught by what is happening further away in their immediate environment. Trips out for babies offer close and affectionate contact between adult and baby. There is also the healthy impact of getting outside, and the stimulation to learning offered through new sights and sounds. If you work in an area with poor air quality, you may want to select your routes with care, but do find some areas to take them to. Younger babies may simply enjoy the movement but, once they can comfortably sit up, older babies are ready to take in the local sights and sounds.

Play and learning tips

You all need to get out sometimes, or else it can seem like a very long day.

Babies are ready to be interested and delighted by what seem like very ordinary outings to adults.

Babies will not be picky about where you go for your local trips, so long as you are on the move and you talk with them. Outings are a shared activity.

Activities

Getting out together

■ Tired, bored or fractious babies are often soothed by the rhythm of being walked in a baby carrier or pushed in a suitable buggy or pram.

■ Babies in a carrier enjoy the contact of being physically close and the reassuring sound of a familiar voice.

■ Talk with babies and pay attention to how they respond. The trip is also a time for personal communication.

■ Make sure that you regularly make warm eye contact with babies. Give a smile and a friendly word. Tell them where you are going and what you are doing. Of course, they will not understand your words but your affectionate tone will involve them.

What can you see?

■ Get down to the eye level of babies in a buggy or pram, not only to communicate with them, but to see the environment as they do.

■ What can they actually see and is it interesting? Will it help to adjust how babies are lying or sitting? Do you regularly need to line up the buggy or pram for an interesting sight?

■ Turn the buggy to face an intriguing shop window or a wonderful display of blossoms. Move the buggy close to something of interest that the babies can swipe at or touch.

■ Stop regularly during a local trip and look with the baby from his angle. Check what has caught his attention and share his visual interest. You give an early boost to babies' sense of self worth when you show pleasure in what has excited them.

■ Invite babies to home in on one or two new sights with 'Oh, look! Do you see the bird on the fence?' or to listen with, 'What's that noise? It's a fire engine. Look here it comes!'

Here we are!

■ By nine or ten months, babies may start to recognise some features of a local circuit.

■ Share their pleasure as they point out a familiar landmark or kick their legs with anticipation as they recognise the last metres before the bakers or getting back to nursery or home.

Development within the second year

Within the months between the first and second birthday, most toddlers move from looking and behaving like a large baby to looking and behaving like a very young child. A toddler's individual temperament is becoming ever clearer and her own wishes are expressed firmly through gestures, other body language and her emerging words. A toddler's close relationship with family and other carers is important to her and she shows both affection to familiar, loved people and distress at separation or new and confusing situations. Toddlers want to feel part of their daily lives, and they can learn much happily through involvement in their daily routines. Of course, they can learn a great deal through play but observant adults who offer, 'Do you want to help me?', discover how much toddlers enjoy being trusted to have a role in domestic events that can seem very mundane to the grown-ups.

A toddler's ability to understand and express herself is supported by adults and older siblings who take her early communications seriously and show interest. By the end of this year, most toddlers will be expressing recognisable words and will show how they understand considerably more than they can say themselves. Alert adults can easily see the impact of a toddler's previous experience on what she does. These very young children show evidence of remembering, and some planning and problem-solving skills. Their play, creative exploration and emerging language is so much more than simple copying of what they have seen someone else do or heard them say.

Toddlers are absorbed in using all their senses and want to practise and extend their physical capabilities. They are inquisitive and open to any appropriate challenges to explore and learn. They do, of course, have a limited understanding of how the world works, because they still have so much to learn. So caring adults need to keep them safe without undue restrictions and to be realistic in their expectations. Adults need great reserves of patience as they help toddlers to learn about where and how they can play and what is off limits to them.

As toddlers cannot yet take care of themselves, adults need to ensure the young children's health and well-being through adequate rest, nutrition, hygiene and emotional care in a calm and secure environment. Adults who value the caring role will help toddlers' all-round development.

Contents

46–50 Developing relationships

51–60 Using the senses

61–68 Language and creative development

69–74 Physical development

75–79 Using the environment

developing relationships

Care of toddlers – a shared task

Developmental focus

An individual response to baby and toddler care offers opportunities for children to share in their own care. Even very young children want to take on small parts of the daily routine for themselves: to push an arm into a sleeve or to hold the spoon at mealtime. They are learning physical skills like co-ordination and the very beginnings of self-reliance. But, equally important, young children are experiencing satisfaction in what they can do, when the adult is as delighted as they are over this development.

Supportive adults value this caring role: both what they do and how they enable the toddler to be a part of daily routines. Toddlers can learn from a regular yet flexible pattern that helps them to understand and so predict a familiar sequence for mealtimes, tidying up or getting clothes on or off again. As well as the importance of toddlers' health and general well being, good physical care also supports their thinking and communication skills when that care is offered within a warm and caring relationship.

Play and learning tips

Value care and caring routines. They matter to toddlers so adults should respect this time as well.

Talk with parents so that you are all up to date with the toddlers' abilities and preferences and so that you offer continuity between home and other settings – especially in events such as toilet training.

Make routines an individual experience for each toddler. Avoid any sense of a conveyer belt attitude to changing or feeding. This attitude is disrespectful to very young children, and it also tends to create cranky and uncooperative toddlers.

As far as you possibly can, organise to provide all physical care and daily routines with time and relaxed attention. You can create a warm and playful atmosphere without inappropriately turning meals or toilet training into playtime as such.

Activities

Feeding

■ Gather everything for feeding before making sure the toddler is comfortable. If you leave her to go and get a spoon or drink she may become unsettled.

■ Try to create a calm and happy atmosphere by smiling, humming or singing while putting on bibs, sitting her down and getting ready.

■ Talk about the food she is about to eat. Name the items she picks up by spoon or finger food. Lick your lips and use enthusiastic words to express enjoyment.

■ Eating together is ideal, as young children are influenced by what they see others eating. Make meal or snack times a social occasion. Sit with toddlers and keep them company, even if you are not always eating at the same time.

■ All young children appreciate attractively-presented food and may well be interested in helping you to arrange the table or a plate of items.

■ If a child is not very enthused about her food, present her sandwich in a novel way. Use shape-cutters to create star- or heart-shaped sandwiches. Pieces of fruit can be placed on the plate to create a funny picture, a face or a car.

■ Never present the toddler with too much on the plate, just have two plates. Finishing one will allow a sense of achievement and then you can encourage her to eat from the next plate.

■ Help her to feed independently by making sure all she needs is within her reach. Encourage her to mirror your actions by showing how to use implements.

Dressing

■ While you are dressing or changing a toddler's clothes, describe what you are doing. Name each piece of clothing as you put it on. Try to follow the same familiar order.

■ Say little rhymes, such as 'where are your fingers?'

■ Let toddlers help to dress or undress themselves. Watch them to see what they can now manage.

Play with clothes

■ Place three pairs of separated socks into a small basket. Ask the toddlers to bring some socks. Repeat this every so often, and eventually they may choose a pair. This can be repeated with shoes, which may be easier.

■ Offer a challenge to the toddler by placing older children's shoes and adult's shoes among her own. Ask her to bring her shoes, or your own shoes. Always offer praise and encouragement.

■ Sit her in her underwear next to a basket or box containing her clothes. Allow her to play with them and try to put them on. Offer praise for trying.

■ Take a piece of fabric or board and attach some fastenings, such as large buttons, Velcro, a heavy-duty zip and stud fastenings. Encourage the toddler to undo them, then fasten them again. Offer help as she wishes.

Keeping clean

■ In the tub or a paddling pool,

encourage toddlers to make movements that will develop arm and leg muscles.

- Experiment with 'swimming' in the tub or pool.
- During the daily routines of washing hands and face, brushing teeth and combing hair, say little rhymes – for example – 'Here we go round the mulberry bush'. Role play the actions, mime an action and let the children copy.
- Let a toddler wash your hands and face, comb your hair, brush your teeth. Provide the play materials for toddlers to pretend to care for dolls or teddies.

Toilet training

- There is no set time for starting training. In conversation with parents, you must judge when an individual child is likely to manage. At some time within the second half of this year, toddlers may show that they are ready to start toilet training, using a potty, small toilet or seat within an ordinary toilet. (Toddlers vary as to what they prefer.) Toilet or potty training can be a difficult time for both adult and child and in the majority of cases it will take a while and include many 'accidents'.
- Try to make the child very familiar with the potty or toilet. Before starting the training, introduce her doll or teddy to the routine.
- Read stories about potty training.
- Use the potty with the child in a quiet place, not surrounded by others. Keep the toddler company, perhaps chat with him while he is on the potty.
- Be as relaxed as possible. Never force toddlers or get angry with them; this only makes the process harder. Some will not be ready until about two years of age.

Sleep and rest time

- Time for quiet, calm and rest should be provided for toddlers. If toddlers are in full day care, they will almost certainly need a sleep at some time.
- If they have a nap during the day, play soft, calm music to help relaxation.
- During play sessions, if you notice a child who is tired or fretful, let him know he can stop playing and sit quietly.
- If you are in a nursery, it is important to have allocated quiet areas for young children. A set area for rest and quiet time should be accessible, with cushions, drapes, soft lighting, rugs, soft toys, blankets and pillows.
- Hang flowers, stars, clouds and ribbons from the drapes for children to watch while they are resting.

The social life of toddlers

Developmental focus

Toddlers will have developed an understanding of who is familiar in their daily life and who is not so well known or a completely new face. They are able to make close relationships with adults within and outside the family and with other children. Toddlers need some predictability and continuity in their lives for healthy social and personal development. Too many changes, or the arrival of unknown carers can block their willingness to make contact – life seems just too uncertain.

Very young children think of themselves as individuals and you need to treat them as such. Clear respect for their individuality will enable toddlers to develop their social self as well. It is a myth that very young children only engage in parallel play. If you watch them, you will see that toddlers make contact with each other, play together and sometimes develop their own simple games with a friend or sibling.

Toddlers are ready to be caring towards others and helpful within the daily routines, although not all the time, of course. Give attention to how you can involve them appropriately and encourage a friendly atmosphere in the group or family home. Young children grow in sensitivity to others when they have experienced a warm concern for their interests and an environment in which they do not have to fight for adult attention. Toddlers can then start to develop what is called prosocial behaviour: the very beginnings of an awareness of the feelings and needs of others and a wish to support them.

Play and learning tips

Talk directly to toddlers and use their names. Treat them in all ways as individuals.

Respect toddlers' cuddlies or special blankets and find out the name that the toddler uses for this significant item. Never ask young children to give over a precious personal item to another child.

In nursery care, take the time to gain the attention of individual children for any suggestions or instructions.

Do not address them as a group, nor expect them to react to whatever name that adults give to the toddler room. They will not realise that you are speaking to them.

Activities

Making friends

- Toddlers can feel secure enough to make sustained social contact with other young children. Watch them and notice the attachments that are developing.
- Help them to learn the names of other children and key people in their lives. Play 'Where's?' spotting games with the names of children and adults.
- Respect the children's preferences rather than assuming that they have made a friend in another child.
- In a home situation young children are sometimes brought together because the adults (childminders, nannies or parents) enjoy each other's company. Do not insist that the children ought to be friends too, because sometimes they may not get along at all.

Playing together

- Give toddlers space and time to develop their own games in which both have a role to play.
- Actively listen and watch toddlers at play and respond positively to their gestures and actions.
- Set up some activities in which more than one child can play together. It might

be very simple dressing up with hats, making faces or funny movements in a large mirror, hide and peek-a-boo games or building up a brick tower and then knocking it down.

Learning to co-operate

■ Sharing does not make much sense to a toddler but giving (when you sometimes are on the receiving as well as the giving end) and trades or swaps can work well.

■ Help children by having enough play materials that turn-taking is not too great an imposition.

■ Have a rich array of recycled materials such as cardboard boxes, tubes, large curtain rings, corks, lidded boxes or tins. Make these available in your treasure basket or create a special time of discovery play, when toddlers may explore singly but often work together.

Finding a social role

■ Toddlers want to be part of what happens and are only too keen to have a helpful role in the domestic routine of the home or nursery.

■ Find safe and achievable tasks that can be shared to show toddlers that you welcome and trust their skills. Let them tidy up with you, fetch you something simple from across the room, hand out banana slices or pat a baby's hand.

■ Always say 'thank you' or 'well done' for the toddlers' help. He will soon follow your good example and express similar warm feelings to others.

■ Look for opportunities to give toddlers choices and the chance to express an opinion through words and gestures. It might simply involve choosing a story or a book or deciding where to stick a picture on a board or wall.

■ Notice and encourage children in their natural concerns for each other.

■ When toddlers tell you someone is crying, respond to their concern and thank them for bringing it to your attention.

■ Affirm their attempts to comfort their peers, for instance, offering a stroke on the hand or fetching another toddler's comfort blanket.

using the senses

Seeing, exploring and understanding

Developmental focus

By twelve months, the older baby's vision is well developed, allowing him to watch and to act upon the world around him. Toddlers' hand-eye co-ordination continues to improve and their ability to walk releases babies' hands, allowing them to manipulate objects freely and sometimes to carry items with them from place to place.

Toddlers are able to focus on close and distant objects – this ability supports them as they recognise familiar faces easily and point to objects and events of interest. With this developing visual awareness, toddlers enjoy looking at simple picture books and touching familiar items on the pages, as well as exploring almost everything in their familiar environment.

Play and learning tips

Looking around and scanning with interest are important aspects of the development of concentration in a very young child. Encourage the growth of this ability without putting undue pressure on toddlers.

Provide plenty of hands-on experience and let toddlers see, as well as feel, the qualities that they will eventually (but not yet!) describe as colour, shape, texture and other abstract concepts.

By all means use the words to describe such ideas but do not press the toddler to try to learn the words.

Very young children are able to and enjoy sorting items out by 'same' and

'different' long before they can link real objects to abstractions like colour. Their looking skills are a vital first step.

Activities

Box games

- Ask your local electrical store or supermarket for large cardboard boxes. These are good for peek-a-boo games.
- Cut interesting shapes all over the box. Let children go inside to peek out and let others peek in.

Well spotted!

- Toddlers are able to start playing 'hide and seek' – let them watch you hiding the first few times until they understand the game.
- Have a rich variety of simple picture books on hand to help develop this interest. With only one, or at most two toddlers, play spotting games for familiar items within a picture or poster.
- Toddlers begin to understand the names of things before they can vocalise them. So use their visual as well as their comprehension skills and ask questions in a playful way such as: 'Where's the...?' and 'What have I done with the...?'
- Try a few deliberate mistakes in familiar routines and ask, 'What's wrong here?'

Coloured frames

- You need cardboard frames of various sizes (15cm x 15cm, 20cm x 20cm and so on), coloured gels or cellophane, and everyday objects such as fruit and toys.
- Tape or glue the gels or cellophane to the cardboard frames. Then encourage the children to hold the frame up to the front of their faces. Or hold it for them.
- Place one item at a time in front of the frame, and let them look at the unusual image. Ask the toddler, 'What is it?' and use the colour word as information, 'It's gone all green!'
- Swap frames so they can look through different colours and ask questions or make comments to stimulate toddlers' interest and their response.
- Allow them to share frames with their friends.
- Extend this activity by making coloured spectacles using cardboard frames and cellophane. Encourage them to play with the glasses on. Alternatively, use sunglasses, making sure they don't have prescription lenses and supervising the children closely.

Silk swatches

- Put various pieces and colours of silk or a similar material in a decorated box or bag.
- Make sure the children are sitting comfortably around the box or bag. Then tell them a story about the 'magic' material inside the box or bag.
- Demonstrate 'juggling' or throwing the material high into the air and watching the silk float slowly to the ground. Extend your arms to catch it.
- Let the children take turns catching the 'magic' material.
- Get the children to place all the silk swatches gently back into the box.

Catch and find

■ Use tissues, soft scarves, balloons or bubbles as objects to watch and then try to catch as they float down.
■ Use bubble makers and help toddlers if they cannot make the bubbles themselves. Throw or roll suitable items, so the toddlers have to watch and track the objects in order to retrieve or catch them (toddlers are still learning to catch so don't make it too hard).

Touch and feel

Developmental focus

Toddlers still put objects into their mouths, but this is now more for exploring taste and texture and often for comfort. They have now learned what many familiar objects feel like – so, without needing to look, they may stretch out for their favourite cuddly, grasp and pull it to them, confident from the feel.

A toddler's skills of touch, combined with more visual confidence, allows her to manipulate objects to see what will happen, and to repeat an action, often many times with obvious delight. With improved hand-eye co-ordination, toddlers can experiment in deliberately bringing objects together, putting small objects into different containers and feeling for relative size and shape.

Toddlers still use and welcome touch as a means of communication. They want to be close to familiar adults, especially if they feel uncertain, tired or unwell. They also use touch to make contact with other children and should be helped to be more gentle if necessary.

Play and learning tips

Toddlers begin to learn about what they should not touch, but it is a slow process.

Be patient and show them what is safe to look at but not to touch. They may even spontaneously learn helpful phrases like 'Not for me', so that they are more able to guide themselves.

Introduce the words for different textures, but do not expect toddlers to learn and remember them yet. Their enjoyable hands-on experience will build the foundation so that the words eventually have real meaning.

Activities

Discovery play

■ Elinor Goldschmied developed her idea of the treasure basket (see page 16) into special play sessions suitable for nurseries. She called this activity 'heuristic play'. This activity is suitable for many of the sections in this book – not only for developing touch as a sense.
■ Gather a wide range of materials, some of which will be similar to what is included in the treasure basket. Find many different types and sizes of container, cardboard or see-through tubes, safe lengths of metal chain, empty cones from knitting machine wool, old-fashioned wooden clothes pegs, large corks, large sponge hair curlers, large wooden curtain rings and other

everyday and recycled natural materials.

- Store the material in large cloth bags or similar that will keep the material dust-free and safe. Bring out the materials once or twice a week as a special play time so that the resource does not become too familiar.
- Lay out the material attractively in a clear space and let the toddlers play and explore as they wish. Look at and enjoy anything that toddlers wish to show you or with which they want your help.
- Relax and value this time as an opportunity to watch and listen to the toddlers.
- Warn them before it is time to tidy up and involve them in this process.

Give, take and find games

- Younger toddlers are still keen to use their skills to give you objects and to take them back again. Be enthusiastic and willing to repeat the game again and again.
- Pretend you are going to keep something with, 'Oh no, it's mine now', or hiding the object in an obvious place (behind your back, under a cloth or under your jumper). Make sure toddlers can tell you are having fun by the tone of your voice and the expression on your face.

Feel and find

- Put four of five familiar objects into a cloth bag and let toddlers feel inside and then bring out the toy, cup, brick or other object.
- Encourage them to feel and think about what they can touch with, 'I wonder what it is?' or 'Is it the ball, then?' Don't press toddlers to guess, although they may start to try.
- When the object emerges, say, 'You touched the cup' or 'you got the spoon'. Join in their interest at which toy they have discovered and have a go yourself – perhaps make a mistake or seem uncertain.

Touch, sound and action

- Walk your fingers towards a toddler and finish with a gentle touch or tickle.
- Play singing games where finger or hand actions and touch are part of the song or rhyme. For instance, 'Round and round the garden, like a teddy bear, one step, two steps, tickle under there', finishing with a gentle or more vigorous tickle, depending on what this toddler prefers.
- Play games like pat-a-cake where touch is part of the exchange.

Feely books

- Make a cloth book with different pages made of varied squares of material.
- Encourage toddlers to feel, stroke and rub the different textures.
- Collect different textures of paper and other similar materials: wallpaper, popper wrap, shiny wrapping paper and stiff brown paper. Let toddlers scrunch up the sheets and then bat them around like a ball.

What does it feel like?

- Let toddlers experience water in its different forms: when it is still, a steady drip or a pour. Feel the difference between wet and dry using a flannel or sponge, material or tissues. What's the difference between warm water, cooler water and ice cubes?

- Blow some bubbles, chase, touch them and feel them pop.
- What does sticky feel like? Test this by feeling a blob of jam, sticky tape or plasters.
- Explore the feel of soft and squishy with play dough. Do not insist that toddlers make something in particular with the dough, just let them feel it in their hands.
- Explore the feel and ways of manipulating mixtures: knead bread or pizza dough or shape and roll biscuit dough. Then cook and eat it too.

Smelling and learning

Developmental focus

Smell seems to be the sense that many adults take most for granted. Yet it is the most direct and basic of our senses. Our own adult sense of smell is connected to memories, sometimes from childhood, and toddlers can also respond to familiar smells – either pleasant or unpleasant. For instance, the smell of an aromatic oil burning in the playroom can remind toddlers of their homes, or the smell of fabric conditioner on a blanket can evoke their own beds. Toddlers will not have the words to explain these links, but the sensation will be part of their daily experience. Their facial expressions, gestures and a few words will tell you they recognise a smell and whether this recognition brings pleasure. Smells may bring unhappiness or uncertainty, for instance toddlers who have spent time in hospital may associate certain smells with ill health or medical procedures.

Just as toddlers will already be showing you that they prefer certain patterns, sounds or textures, they will also be very particular about smells. Their development will be supported when you provide toddlers with new experiences to explore a variety of smells. Although smell is important to toddlers, they can find the act of deliberately smelling something quite difficult. Often if children are asked to smell something they will blow out through their noses. It is useful to teach the child to blow out through their mouths so that they will breathe in automatically through their noses.

Play and learning tips

Before doing any smell activities with toddlers, check with parents if the children have allergies or sensitivities to any of the objects you plan to use.

If so, place the perfumes, petals and so on, on small sticky backed address labels.

Also talk with parents so that you can be aware if the toddler has had any experiences, such as medical procedures, that could make them unhappy about particular smells. You need to be ready to reassure the young child.

Explain to parents what you are doing and encourage them to enjoy ordinary aromas with their toddlers.

Activities

Enjoy the smells

■ Make a treasure basket with citrus fruit (oranges, lemons, limes). Pierce them with a fork to produce a stronger smell. You could also include wooden fruit and pine cones.

■ Offer the children empty containers in which the smells of, for instance, cosmetics, shampoo and bubble bath, still linger. Let children play with a variety of herbs and flowers with smells that will linger on their hands.

Everyday aromas

■ Encourage children to use their sense of smell on everyday experiences and materials, for instance, food and drink, common toiletries in your setting or toothpaste.

■ Make fruit juice, and encourage the children to smell and taste the fruit. Sometimes prepare food with the children and let them smell the jam or butter, tomatoes or fresh bread.

■ Alert toddlers to smells that signal events in the day, such as 'I smell lunch coming' or 'We're going to have cake for tea, can you smell it cooking?'

Pretty-smelling pictures

■ Gather together a selection of fresh herbs or flower petals. Put them into small tubs and secure the top.

■ Let the children smell each tub. Put a little of each herb (or petal) into the child's hand.

■ Let them sprinkle the herbs (or petals) onto a piece of paper. Alternatively, let them sprinkle the herbs (or petals) onto pre-glued paper and let the children smell and touch their pictures.

Washing hands

■ Place three bottles of scented soap with different odours on a table. Place a blob of each – one at a time – onto your own hand. Invite the toddler to smell each scent.

■ Place a small amount onto the toddler's hands, gently rub into her palms and encourage her to smell the soap. Talk about the smell and feel of the soap while rubbing and rinsing the bubbles from her hands.

■ When dry, ask her to smell her hands again. Can she still smell the scent?

■ Let the toddler choose her favourite soap with which to wash her hands. Alternatively, wash each hand with a different scent.

■ Put some of the soap into a small container of water, allow the toddler to swish the water until bubbles appear, let her place a piece of paper or material over the bubbles, then smell the print.

Out in the garden

■ Buy or borrow some pots or boxes of herbs. Let the toddlers hold or lean over the pots, while you comment on the smells.

■ Encourage the toddlers to smell each of the herbs. Let them touch and feel the herbs, rubbing the leaves to make the

scent stronger and let the smell linger on their hands.

- Allow each child to select and pick one or two herbs and place them in a pot or wrap them in damp tissue to take home.

Natural smells

- Plant ready-potted small herbs or flowers with definite scents. Involve the toddlers to help water and care for the special garden and to smell the plants as they grow.
- Use the children's selection of herbs during a baking activity.
- Go on a woodland walk and let the children experience the smells of leaves, bark, logs or wood shavings. As some country smells are not pleasant, accept that the toddlers may show their disfavour.
- Go on a seashore walk to experience smells such as seaweed or fish.

Mystery labels

- Dip small pieces of tissue (2cm square) into a selection of items such as fabric conditioner, toothpaste, fruit juice, chocolate powder, perfume, vinegar or garlic powder.
- Using sticky-backed address labels, place each of the pieces of tissue between the backing and the label.
- Ask the children to smell the labels and see if they can identify any smells. Leave the raw ingredients out to give the children a clue if needed.
- Which smells do they like best? Which ones don't they like?
- Encourage toddlers' language development with your own comments but bear in mind that even adults often don't have a wide range of words beyond 'nice' and 'nasty' for describing smells.
- If the children enjoy this activity, extend the range of smells. Try tracking down the source of a smell, like toothpaste or ginger biscuits, to the part of your setting where the item is usually kept.

Hearing and listening

Developmental focus

Toddlers need to develop their ability to listen, since this skill, along with looking, forms crucial building blocks for their ability to concentrate. Unlike babies, whose attention is often naturally distracted from one object to another, toddlers can focus very deliberately on items and events of interest. They often want to repeat, or have you repeat, something interesting again and again. If you are willing to follow their request, then you will promote their development, since toddlers learn with repetition and practice.

A toddler is skilled at listening to language, and sways in time to words during singing. They are able to distinguish well between voices and sounds and can recognise simple tunes that have been sung many times by a parent or carer. Having found his voice, a toddler is eager to use it. When you talk with and listen to toddlers, they will support their language development and they will add to their vocabulary and expressive sounds. Speech is a social skill within toddlers' development, so it is aided by listening and responding to adults or older siblings.

Play and learning tips

Toddlers can focus very deliberately on items and events of interest. They learn with repetition and practice, so be ready to 'do it again!'

Provide toddlers with activities that allow them to explore and experiment with new sounds. Combine some familiar and some unfamiliar sounds so toddlers can recognise old favourites as well as novel sounds.

Create an interesting sound environment with rich opportunities for listening to a variety of voices, words and sounds.

Ensure that everyone can hear and be heard in your setting. Avoid continuous background noise and make sure that no adults develop the bad habit of shouting or calling from a distance.

Make sure you have a toddler's attention before you speak or show something of interest. Use his name, hold up your hand or a finger or say kindly, 'Listen now'.

Activities

Sound spotting

- Have a good store of rhymes that become familiar to toddlers so that they can recognise and respond to the opening sounds or words. Add to your repertoire by asking parents to share their rhymes and songs.
- Whenever possible, draw the children's attention to noises and sounds that have meaning in daily life: the sound of the lunch trolley in the hallway, a baby crying in the next room or a police siren out on the road.
- Challenge them to hear or pick out a noise among many different sounds.
- Provide them with play materials that make noises, sounds or tunes.
- Sometimes just sit in peaceful silence in the home, garden or playroom for short periods of time. What can you hear?

Shake, rattle and ring

- For this activity, you will need a sheet of plywood, and items such as a bicycle bell, motor horn, door bell, buzzer and door knocker.

- Attach all the items to the front of the board, making sure they are secure.
- Invite the toddlers to have a look and try the items out.
- Once the children have had time to explore the noises, you can join in. Resist showing the children how to carry out the activity. They will have much more fun finding out by themselves.
- Have a basket with duplicate items that the children can play with too.

Grab a noise

- Collect a variety of fabrics, such as fake fur, kite fabric, foil, bubble wrap, a length of cotton wool, sand paper and cellophane.
- Place the fabric in a large box. Then sit the toddlers down beside the box and invite them to look at what is inside.
- Take one piece of fabric out at a time. Let the children take the fabric and squash it and pull it. Alternate the fabric, bringing out one that will make a noise, then one that will be silent.

When to worry

During this year, it will become clear that some toddlers are not fully confident in using their senses. Although it can be hard to assess visual or hearing loss in young children, it should now be more possible to pin down potential worries.

- Talk with parents, listening to any concerns that they express and sharing your own observations.
- Toddlers with partial or total visual loss will benefit from adjusted play activities as well as your awareness of how not being able to see will affect how they can understand their world
- In the usual course of events, toddlers should be using some words that are recognisable to familiar carers and should be responding to meaningful sounds. If this development is not happening, then hearing loss has to be one explanation to be considered.
- Be aware of toddlers who have many colds, especially if this includes ear infections. The bouts of ill health can mean that their hearing is intermittent, which confuses their learning. Frequent ear infections can directly damage hearing.
- Continue to be aware, with toddlers' parents, of any possible allergies or sensitivities that emerge through exploration of touch and smell.

■ Encourage children to make a noise with each of the fabrics. Describe the feel and the sound it makes as children experiment.
■ Once all the fabrics are out, let the children play with them freely.

Noisy fun

■ Sit two or three toddlers down beside you in a quiet place and make different sounds for their entertainment.
■ For instance, cough gently, saying 'excuse me' and covering your mouth. Keep coughing gently. Pretend to sneeze and invite the children to join the game. Blow a raspberry and ask if they can do this.
■ Make a variety of noises, such as 'oohh', 'aahh' and 'eehh', and encourage the children to copy.
■ Make the noises quietly at first, then louder and louder, then quietly again.
■ Say hello in a funny voice and encourage children to copy.
■ Copy any funny sounds that the toddlers want to make.

Rock and pop

■ Record one-minute extracts from four songs of different styles, such as classical, rock, jazz and country, on a tape.
■ Ask the children to lie on the floor in a space of their own and listen quietly to the music. Then have the children sit up.
■ Play the music again, letting them bob about or get up and move around.
■ Play the music again, encouraging the children to respond in their own way.
■ Watch whether they seem to like some extracts more than others. Ask parents whether the toddlers have any favourite music at home, or current popular songs that they have heard and liked.

language and creative development

Early communication

Developmental focus

A toddler's vocalisations slowly become words because familiar adults and older siblings respond with enthusiasm to those sounds that are close to real words. Many toddlers' first words appear somewhere between twelve to eighteen months, but this varies a great deal. Toddlers are growing in their understanding as well as their ability to express themselves. They need adults who communicate clearly with toddlers, giving them time and patience and help them to link familiar words and phrases with events of the day.

Words are learned because they are useful to the toddler and carry meaning in their environment: the names of people and objects and words like 'more' or 'no' that help the toddler to control what happens. Toddlers use a small number of words but they convey a lot of meaning because of the supporting gestures and expressions. Toddlers' mistakes in how they use words are usually logical; perhaps all furry animals are a 'cat'. Listen and watch the toddlers and you will usually be able to track, with interest, how they have made their sensible errors. Towards the end of this year, many toddlers start to combine two words.

Play and learning tips

Respond to toddlers' full attempts at communication: to the actual words but also to sounds that are close to words and all their expressive gestures.

Give them time and attention so they do not feel rushed.

You will help by saying words clearly and correctly, so toddlers can hear and copy as they wish. But it is not helpful to correct toddlers by making them say words again.

If toddlers are hearing more than one language, they will learn to be bilingual, helped by adults who speak the language that is most fluent for them. Talk with parents so you can understand what the toddler is learning and then you may be able to recognise some words from the language in which you are not fluent.

Activities

Let's have a chat

- Toddlers enjoy short conversations with adults who are genuinely interested. Give your full attention, listen to what the toddler says and watch all the gestures that add to her meaning.
- Expand what she says with a few words of your own. Keep your questions simple, friendly and linked with what interests the toddler and what is visually obvious to her.
- Toddlers believe that you know everything they do. So conversations with their parents can help you to make sense of interesting events or people that you do not know.
- Help toddlers to communicate with each other. Let them try to make contact before speaking up on their behalf. Enjoy their give-me games and other play by watching from the sidelines.

Make the links

- Support children as they begin to communicate the connections they are making with their world through words or gestures and other behaviour.
- Be pleased when a toddler shows how she has remembered the word for something with, 'Well done. That's where we keep the crayons. Which ones would you like?'
- In the second half of this year, toddlers begin to link the picture of something with the real object. Be ready to help this process as you look at books and posters, 'Yes, there's a banana. That's one of your favourites' or 'It's the big red bus. We saw one of those this morning.'

What comes next?

- Share books with a simple and repetitive story line that toddlers can join in and start to anticipate. Start a repeated phrase, pause and let toddlers fill in the words if they want.
- Develop your own story line to tell with books of pictures or photographs without a text.
- Share books with no more than two toddlers, at most three. They are distracted in larger groups.
- Enjoy familiar songs and rhymes with gestures that toddlers can anticipate as you do them and they will soon join in as well. They will ask for a song by a few

words or the gestures of a rhyme.

- Involve toddlers in the daily routine so that they can learn about sequences (what do we do next?) and predict what is needed, by helping you lay the table for lunch or tidy up ready for tea.
- Make plenty of materials available for them to enact this experience in their pretend play.
- Local trips help toddlers recall a route and look ahead. They will enjoy the anticipation of 'Here comes the post box. Are you ready with the letters to post?' and 'Yes, there's our special big tree. Do you think we'll see the squirrel today?'

Spotting games

- Sharpen up toddlers' looking skills and their understanding of useful words with finding games.
- Make a collection of familiar toys and objects and play 'Where's the...?' so toddlers point out or bring the cup, ball or doll.
- You can play the same game with parts of the body. Be enthusiastic and say, 'Yes, well done, that's your nose!'
- Within the second half of the year, toddlers will enjoy looking, spotting and naming with simple pictures or wall posters. Encourage them with comments like, 'Let's find the...', 'Where's the..., I wonder' or 'What's that in the corner there?'

Artistic toddlers

Developmental focus

Toddlers are interested in creative activities because such play satisfies their wish to use their physical skills and to experience through all their senses. They are also intrigued by their ability to make something happen, either to make interesting marks, to squeeze play dough or to create a simple collage that is then displayed and admired. Toddlers relish and learn from the creative process and they need to be given scope to use materials as they wish, within the confines of safety, of course.

Toddlers are ready for mark-making with short, fat, non-toxic crayons that are easy for their hands to grasp and that provide immediate results. Thick paintbrushes or foam wedges are easier for them to hold and give scope for satisfying sweeps of colour and texture. In using play dough or suitable clay, toddlers may sometimes make something, but often learn a great deal through simply manipulating, pushing and poking at the materials.

Play and learning tips

Get any creative activity ready, so that toddlers do not have to wait about or queue for their turn; they will soon lose interest. Let them stop an activity when they have had enough, then they will be ready to be involved another day.

Display some of the toddlers' creations that they want to have shown but do not push young children into producing something for your own adult display. Take photos instead to show how everyone enjoyed an activity.

Keep toddlers' drawings or paintings if they wish and hold onto, or give to parents a selection of what the young children have spontaneously created. Children will enjoy looking at 'my baby drawings' in years to come.

Toddlers can be very pleased with their creations but they will decide in their own time whether a painting or dough model is something in particular. It is unwise to try to push this development by asking toddlers, 'What have you drawn?'. Just admire it.

Activities

Art made easy

- When a young child is first given a crayon he will investigate it by biting, tasting and banging before making marks. Within safety limits, let him explore this material.
- Tape paper to the floor and let toddlers make marks on it with thick crayons.
- Tape a length of string to crayons and attach the string to a table leg so that toddlers don't use the markers on other pieces of furniture or on the walls. Alternatively just watch them closely and stay involved in the activity.
- Gather large cardboard boxes with no lids which a toddler can sit in. Let him decorate the boxes.
- As an alternative to bottled paint, make a thick paste from cornflour, water and food colouring. Give them a small tray of this paste to draw in with a short piece of doweling.
- Make marks on fabric using a range of materials – ask parents to donate old tablecloths or sheets. Use the design to drape over a display table.

Taking art outdoors

- Fill shallow trays with a mixture of powder paint and sand.
- Take the trays outdoors and encourage the children to draw in the sand with their fingers.
- They can shake the trays to erase their drawings and to start a new one.

My book of pictures

- Store each child's pictures in a large spiral-bound notebook, placing a picture on every second page. Cut the blank pages into five horizontal sections.
- Let the toddlers peel back the sections one at a time to eventually reveal the whole picture.

Use blackboards

- Set up a blackboard at the children's level and provide a range of chalks for them to use.
- Paint an area of the wall at the children's height with blackboard paint – it can always be repainted.

Paint dippers

- Cut squares of material 15cm x 15cm, place cotton wool and piece of sponge in the middle, gather corners and tie up into a small sack shape with string.
- Pour some paint into a paper plate for them and show toddlers how to dip in their paint applicators and then print onto the paper.
- Crumpled paper or cotton wool balls

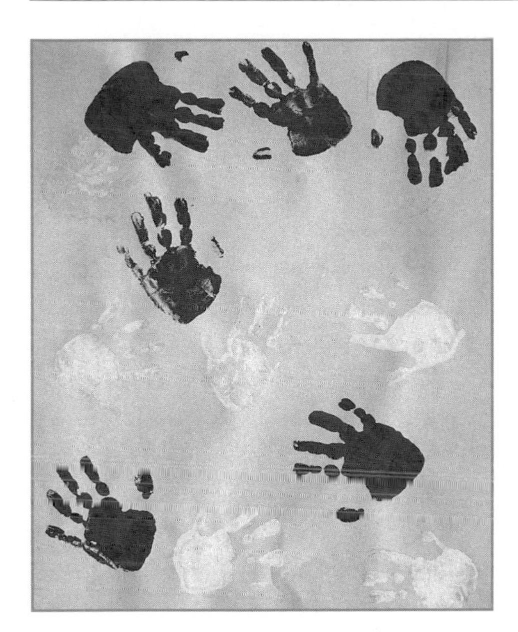

can be used as an alternative. To add texture empty satsuma bags may be used rather than pieces of cloth.

Finger-painting

■ Clear a tabletop at the children's height or sit them on the floor. Let them explore the texture of the paint with their fingers. Encourage them to use their fingers, fingernails, fingertips, knuckles, thumbs and palms to produce different effects.

■ Try variations around this creative theme. You could add aromas, for example – cinnamon, lemon essence or washing-up liquid. Add textures: sand, tea-leaves, woodcarvings or desiccated coconut. Add colour with powder paint, poster paint or glitter.

■ Use alternative materials. Try finger painting with instant pudding mixes, hand lotion or shaving foam.

■ Paint onto different types of paper such as embossed wallpaper, corrugated card and newsprint.

■ Finger-paint directly on to the tabletop then take a print of it using a large sheet of paper.

Pasta collage

■ Gather a range of types of pasta: shells, bows or spirals. Select the bigger sizes, as these are easier for toddlers to manipulate. Let the children put glue on to paper and create their own design with the pasta.

■ The pasta can be coloured by adding a few drops of food colouring and shaking them together to mix.

■ Rice, lentils, dried peas and many other dried foods can be used for collages too – and the sticky side of sticky-backed plastic can be used as a base for younger children to create a collage on. This prevents the need for glue.

Smelly crayons

■ Make crayons by mixing four cups of soap powder with half a cup of water and a range of food colours. Roll them into ping-pong sized balls and leave to dry overnight. Store in an airtight container. Then dip the smelly crayons in a water tray and show toddlers how to scribble on paper. Encourage them to smell as well as look at their creations.

Musical toddlers

Developmental focus

Toddlers will most likely start to use words within this age range and they enjoy sound-making, rhyme and rhythm. Some toddlers will enjoy trying to sing parts of songs, others may mouth or whisper the words. Many toddlers will indicate that they want a favourite sound or piece of music even if they do not have the exact words. Toddlers may also become so focused on the actions for songs that they won't sing along, being more interested in the hand or body movements. Each child will develop at a different rate, but all enjoy and have an interest in musical sound-making and listening.

Play and learning tips

Let parents and carers know the songs and rhymes you are using in the nursery by photocopying them onto attractively-decorated fliers so that the children can enjoy them at home too.

If you live in a diverse community, families may be a rich source of music and song from different cultural backgrounds. Tapes and CDs can still help you select musical resources to reflect the broader multicultural society for all children.

Provide a wide range of opportunities for singing, listening and moving to music, as well as using instruments to create sound. Consider making musical push-and-pull toys as well as using bought musical instruments or sound toys.

Activities

Sing along

■ Use songs as a way to learn about parts of their bodies, for instance, 'Head, shoulders, knees and toes', 'If you're happy and you know it' or 'The hokey cokey'. Make songs personal by using the children's names.

Paper shakers

■ Give out large paper bags and encourage the children to decorate them using large marker pens.

■ Put a small amount of rice, lentils, beans or peas in the bags.

■ Tie the bags with wool, making sure you leave plenty of room for the items inside to move around. Then let the children shake the bags. Comment on the sounds that emerge.

Curtain up!

■ Attach a wooden or metal curtain pole or something similar to a space of wall at a height that gives toddlers easy access.

■ Attach a variety of sound-making objects to the pole. Make them secure and without loose strands.

■ Choose items that can be shaken, knocked, bashed or banged and that will make a selection of sounds. Possibilities include a string of bells or beads, four wooden clothes pegs on a string, conkers, small metal spoons, a whisk, an empty plastic bottle and a plastic bottle with lentils or rice inside.

■ Change the items regularly so the toddlers' interest is held and they revisit the area.

Song box

■ When you introduce children to new songs, it is helpful if they have something visual to recognise and link with the song. Use a large, bright box to store a visual aid for each song. It is more stimulating if the visual aids are 3-D, for example, soft toys, dolls, puppets or models.

- Introduce the object at the same time as the song. The children will begin to realise that the cuddly brown dog means they are invited to sing the song 'How much is that doggy?'.
- Create a box with three or four items that support songs the children know. You might have a padded star for 'Twinkle, twinkle', a rag doll for 'Miss Polly', a plastic duck for 'Five little ducks' and a spider puppet for 'Incey wincy spider'.

Tell me a story

Developmental focus

Stories can become a valued part of the day for toddlers, who enjoy choosing and listening to familiar stories and some new ones. Toddlers relish books shared and read out loud by an adult, but they also like simple storytelling without a book. Stories can also be told through songs, poems and rhymes.

Repetition within a story and hearing favourite stories many times help even very young children to anticipate, recall and join in as they wish. Old favourites may be learned almost by heart and simple tales told to photo or picture books may even be repeated meaningfully by toddlers as they look through the book on their own. The rhythm of a good story or rhyme continues to support toddlers in their language development and crucial listening skills.

Play and learning tips

Make stories a personal time, with close attention to one or two toddlers.

Offer stories and story songs when toddlers ask, or welcome this activity when you suggest it, or simply break into song when you are sitting together.

Help toddlers to learn to care for books by showing them how to turn pages and by not leaving out easily-torn books. Gently remove books that are treated as objects to throw or suck on.

Keep special books in a container, especially those with pulls or more delicate features. Bring them out regularly and look at them with toddlers. Make sturdy books easily available on a low shelf or container.

Activities

Recognising and asking for stories

- Look for every opportunity to respond to the choice of an individual child at the time that he or she wants a story.
- Watch out for how individual children ask for a known story. They may bring you the book they want, use one or two words that hint at the title or may try a gesture from a story song's hand movements.
- Keep a record of the stories that the toddlers request and see how it changes over time.
- Take some photos of toddlers enjoying

the stories. Enjoy the photos now and with parents, but also keep them safe for the child to enjoy when a little older, as part of the personal story of 'what I did when I was little'.

Telling a tale to pictures

- In books with just photos or drawings, create your own story-line and tell the same sequence each time.
- Keep it simple, with some examples of 'Ooh look at...' or 'Where's...?' Try an anticipatory 'And then...' or 'I wonder what will happen...' as you turn the page.
- Look for opportunities to build familiar sounds into your story-line: cats that meow, cows that moo or babies who cry.
- Listen in when children choose to look at this book on their own; you may well hear some of the story you created.
- Be ready to share a special story-line with colleagues and parents, because young children are likely to require the 'proper' story told to the pictures.

Tell it again!

- Children learn stories by hearing them many times, perhaps three to four times in succession at the same sitting.
- Be responsive to the children – they will learn from more repetitions than you would probably choose. Be just as expressive each time you tell or sing the story.
- Try to follow the individual child's lead or allow each child sitting with you to have his or her own turn at saying, 'Again!'.
- Pause at appropriate times in the telling of a tale, especially where there is a sense of 'What's coming next?'. Give the children a chance to join in, if they wish, by repeating a phrase or question that forms part of many good stories.

Stories through rhyme and song

- Add steadily to the children's repertoire of story songs and rhymes and learn new ones whenever you can from parents.
- Mobile toddlers may enjoy more active movements such as in 'Incey Wincy Spider', 'Ring-a-ring-a-roses' or 'I'm a little teapot'.
- Be ready to repeat a new, well-liked story rhyme several times so that the children feel they have got to know it well.
- Let children join in as they want and do not put any pressure on them about performing. Some children will simply enjoy listening, watching and anticipating what will happen next.

Enjoying books

- Make books easily available to the children, on a low shelf or table or in a broad open container.
- Sometimes join a child who is sitting with a book and look too. The child will then feel comfortable to offer you a book and indicate he would like to hear a story.

physical development

Energetic and on the move

Developmental focus

Toddlers have now developed considerable physical control compared with their baby months. Some may be walking confidently before or soon after their first birthday, while others may need to be encouraged to begin. The timing of the first steps varies a great deal, and it is important to encourage toddlers through all the physical successes that happen before walking. Pulling up to stand, walking while holding on to furniture for support and tottering along while adults hold their hands are all exciting events for a toddler.

Toddlers need and want plenty of varied play experiences during which they can strengthen their arms, legs and body muscles. Their physical development is promoted when they have safe space and equipment to allow them to crawl, climb, walk, throw things and balance. Toddlers enjoy pushing and pulling wheeled toys and propelling themselves along on pedal toys such as bikes and tractors. They learn and practise the balance to pick up toys and carry them around, and they are keen to start negotiating stairs and simple climbing frames.

Toddlers need to be watched to

keep them safe, and plenty of encouragement from adults who are as excited as they are about their achievements. Bursts of energy are normal for this age group, and toddlers who are kept restricted or made to be 'quiet' will respond by persistent activity that adults may inappropriately criticise as 'naughty'. Some toddlers are by temperament more wary or daunted by a tumble; they especially need caring adults to support them, offer practical help, like holding a hand, and emotional support to build up their confidence.

Play and learning tips

Offer safe space and plenty of practice – toddlers need to repeat actions and gain confidence over the weeks and months.

Value the importance of physical development for toddlers. Their increasing skills open up the world for them, enabling them to explore without your assistance and to bring items and events excitedly to your attention.

Use of physical skills, in play or within ordinary daily routines, can give toddlers immense pleasure and satisfaction. Watch them and you will see how important these skills are in the toddlers' personal world.

Activities

Fun in using skills

- Supply cardboard boxes large enough for toddlers to climb into and out of again. They will enjoy this activity and it will help to promote co-ordination and balance.
- Provide wheeled toys that children can sit on to develop steering skills, balance and co-ordination.
- Organise outings to parks where children can use suitable play equipment or simply have fun running, jumping and shouting in the open air.
- Make sure there is a soft surface such as mats, sand or grass under any climbing toys. Soft surfaces are also important for gentle 'wrestling' games.

Ball games

- Provide balls of all sizes and of various materials to stimulate toddlers to move around and practise chasing, grabbing and holding.
- Roll a ball towards a toddler from across the room. Encourage the child to bend over, pick it up, and bring it back to you. Give a big hug and applause to motivate the child further.
- Put a large, soft ball in the middle of the play area. Kick the ball gently to demonstrate. Then encourage the toddlers to have a go. You may want to hold the ball yourself if they are still unsteady on their feet.
- Encourage toddlers to move the ball in other ways, like pushing, rolling or shoving it along.

Throw it in the hole

- Cut out a large hole in a cardboard box and place it in the middle of the floor along with balls or bean bags.
- Encourage toddlers to drop or throw them into the hole. Cheer when they 'score'.

Walking games

- When children have learned to walk, there are many games you can encourage them to play to increase their co-ordination.
- You could walk in different ways – either backwards, forwards, marching, walking on tiptoes. Walk slowly and walk fast. Hop, skip, jump and run.
- Pretend to be different animals that toddlers are likely to know. For example, move as slow as a snail or gallop like a horse.
- Provide pull-along toys to encourage children to walk for a longer period.

Balloons

- Tie balloons to string and hang them up in the middle of the room, at a height so that children can reach them easily.
- Show them how to hit the balloons and make them swing.
- Make up games such as getting children to stand at the side of the room, run to the balloons and bat them with their hands and run back again.
- Dancing with balloons can be encouraged by giving each child two balloons on short ribbons. They can twirl them, bang them together or bounce them on the floor or grass.

Chasing games

- Play running or crawling chasing games with toddlers. Make sure you move slowly enough that they can get away sometimes and can catch you.
- Blow bubbles and encourage the children to chase them around the room and catch them.

Poking, piling and filing

Developmental focus

With increased fine motor control, toddlers can start to pick up small objects and manipulate them in a deliberate way. For example, they start to build small towers from blocks, manage very simple jigsaws and enjoy putting smaller objects into larger ones and tipping them out again, often many times.

Toddlers like to use their physical skills to join in their own care and this beginning to self-reliance can give them a lot of pleasure. They may be able to pull off their socks or hat, or perhaps

pull up loose trousers. They are more able to feed themselves, manage drinks through a straw or suitable cup and control dribbling or drooling.

Fine physical skills are reflected in toddlers' play as they develop the ability to grasp crayons using their whole hand to make marks on paper. They may be able to handle a large paint brush when given the opportunity. Toddlers' interest in books gives them the opportunity to turn pages, usually several at a time, and to recognise and point to items on the page.

Play and learning tips

Provide interesting and varied play materials that enable toddlers to apply and practise their growing abilities.

Look for the many opportunities within daily routines and sharing in their own care, as well as play activities.

Share useful skills and information such as which way up to hold a book and how to be careful with books and other more delicate materials.

Provide a wide variety of materials that allow toddlers to exercise their interest and skills in picking up and putting down, sorting, making piles, putting into containers and carrying around. (See also discovery play on page 53.)

Activities

Fine finger work

- Provide the children with empty, large cardboard boxes, which they can scribble on, inside and out, with crayons.
- When reading books with toddlers, encourage them to point to and identify specific, recognisable items on the page.
- Place large basters in a tray or basin of water and encourage the children to squeeze the water in and out of the basters.
- Tie a toy to the child's high chair with a piece of elastic – this will encourage him to pull it up after having thrown it off.
- Hang a blackboard within the children's reach, encouraging them to make marks with chalks. Alternatively, paint an area with blackboard paint – it is possible to paint over it again.

Wonder boxes

- Collect a range of colourful boxes and put interesting objects inside them, such as a variety of shells, coloured glass pebbles, a collection of plastic animals or a miniature tea set.
- Allow the children to take the lids off the boxes and handle the objects.

Bringing the post

- Ask parents and carers to bring in old

junk mail and make a letter-box by painting an empty box red and cutting a slot in it.

■ Let the children enjoy posting the mail through the slot and then allow them to empty the letter-box and 'deliver' the mail elsewhere in the nursery.

■ Wrap up toys with paper or cloth material and encourage the children to unwrap them to see what's inside.

Finger fishing

■ Set up a basin or tray of water and cut out small fish shapes from a range of interesting materials.

■ Get the children to 'fish' out the pieces of materials using only their forefingers and thumbs.

■ You can vary the experience by changing the temperature of the water, or adding bubble bath or non-staining food colouring.

Pasta chains

■ Gather a range of uncooked pasta shapes that can be easily threaded on to lengths of string – for example, macaroni, penne or cannelloni.

■ Help the children to paint the pasta shapes and then cut lengths of string for them to thread the pasta shapes on to. Help them as much as they wish – this is a fine, detailed task.

■ Allow them to wear their home-made jewellery and, if they wish, make a display of their creative work.

Manipulative play

■ Help develop the toddlers' fine motor skills by placing a range of malleable materials in a basin or sand tray. Choose materials that they can hold, squeeze, pull apart, poke, bash and roll.

■ Ensure a variety of experiences by changing the malleable materials and tools regularly.

■ Play dough is always popular with toddlers as well as older children. Add food colouring to brighten it up, essences to give it a fragrance or glitter, rice or sand to give it a texture. Gloop is another popular option.

Holiday suitcase

■ Fill an old suitcase with sand and allow the children to play with it using sieves, funnels, buckets and spades.

■ Replace the sand with cereal or rice.

Leaves are falling

■ Take the children on a walk outdoors.

■ Encourage them to play with leaves – picking them up, throwing them, scrunching them or dropping them one at a time.

Push the cork

■ Decorate used formula milk tins attractively. Cut a 'hole' in the plastic lid that is just big enough for wine bottle corks to fit through.

■ Gather a collection of used corks and encourage the toddlers to push them through the hole. Allow them to remove the lid and empty the corks out. (Do not let them suck or chew on the corks).

Peg race

- Place a selection of bright clothes pegs into a basket.
- Let the toddlers explore and experiment with them.
- Take a few pegs and, one at a time, 'snap' one on to the side of the basket. Offer the toddler a peg encouraging him to try the 'snap'.
- Alternatively, place the basket in front of the toddler with all the pegs 'snapped' to the side. Encourage him to 'unsnap' them in the basket.

Vegetable preparation

- Place corn-on-the-cob and pea pods in bowls on a table. Show the children other bowls containing single peas and corn kernels.
- Invite them to prepare the food, offering a few pods or cob of corn. Help them by popping open the pea pods.
- This food can later be cooked to have in soup or with some rice, or fresh peas can be eaten raw.
- Try this activity with other foods that can be handled and prepared.

using the environment

Getting outside

Developmental focus

Mobile toddlers want to explore the outdoors in their own way. They are fascinated by outdoor events and objects that may seem very ordinary to you. Watch toddlers and you will see how ready they are to be intrigued and enchanted. Toddlers are soon able to learn words to name what they see and will use their emerging language to tell you about what interested them. They are learning about the world around them, what happens and how they can sometimes be involved.

Toddlers have no understanding of potential danger or hygiene issues, but it is possible to start their learning about care and cleanliness without restricting their explorations too much. They will respond to kindly suggestions like 'look but don't touch' for some objects.

Play and learning tips

Move around the garden or yard with toddlers at their pace. They cannot learn if they are rushed.

Show an interest in what has caught their attention. Tune into what they want to watch or touch and they will learn far more than if it is always you who decides what is interesting.

Obviously, if any children have allergies or a tendency to sneeze at pollen or seeds, then change the activities accordingly.

Activities

Look and touch

■ You may think stones are boring but toddlers are often fascinated by them. Gently stop them putting anything into their mouths and, if need be, arrange for a pile of smooth stones and shells that you washed earlier.

- Gently encourage children to touch and smell flowers or leaves. Plant some aromatic herbs like lavender, rosemary or lemon balm to smell.
- In the autumn, watch the falling leaves or seeds like sycamore 'helicopters' and blow on the white dandelion seed heads.
- If your garden has no trees, bring in a big bag of clean leaves. The children can kick the leaves, hurl handfuls into the air and throw themselves into the soft pile.

Minibeast safari

- Find out where the mini-beasts live in your garden and soon the toddlers will revisit their 'homes'. Show the children how to just watch rather than poke or scoop up.
- Lift a few large stones for the toddlers and watch what scurries out. Turn over the earth with the child's help and watch for the worms.
- Keep an eye out for spiders' webs so you can watch them at work. Enjoy the magical sight of sunlight sparkling through dew on the web.
- A feeder in the tree can encourage birds to visit your garden and stay long enough for children to see them clearly and recognise regular visitors.

On the move

- Create the space in your garden for toddlers to get moving with push along tricycles and other wheeled vehicles.
- Provide small wheelbarrows for transporting any outdoor toys as well as some of the piles of leaves. The wheelbarrow is ideal when toddlers help to tidy up the garden.
- A store of large cardboard boxes can be anything the children imagine, as well as providing the fun of climbing in, sitting down, getting up and out, again and again.

Games in the garden

- Big balls and ones that bounce easily allow children to practise their skills of throwing, rolling and passing a ball.
- Play peek-a-boo around garden obstacles and simple hide-and-seek games. You have to pretend not to see the toddlers with 'Where's Jamie now?' and 'Where has Ayesha gone? I can't see her anywhere!'
- Running games start with a '1,2,3 go!' Chasing games can end in a big hug and swing up in the air for the child. Sometimes toddlers will chase you. Run slowly so that they can catch you. Experiment with fast and slow walking, turns to each side, big and little strides and walking backwards.
- Walk toddlers one at a time around the garden with their feet resting on yours.

Some splashing ideas

Developmental focus

Toddlers' physical skills now enable them to work with water themselves: pushing around the floating objects, learning to pour and to manipulate different containers and other water toys. They are often fascinated by water and will watch natural sources as well as water-based play activities. Play with water and other suitable materials will support toddlers as they learn about the world and patterns of cause and effect.

Play and learning tips

When toddlers are confident to stand and move about independently, they enjoy playing at the water tray. A large plastic washing-up bowl is fine if you work in a family home.

Think beyond a water tray and look at daily routines for opportunities for toddlers to learn.

Toddlers have a very limited understanding of danger. They can be harmed by excessively hot water, chilled by very cold and at risk of drowning from even shallow water sources. Watch them and be close.

Activities

Water power

- Toddlers love pouring from one container into another. Their often repetitive play is a good way for them to practise this skill when spillages do not matter.
- Provide containers with some holes, plastic sieves or small cutlery drainers so that toddlers can watch the water trickle out the bottom. Add bath toys to your collection at the water tray or bowl.
- Help them to build a small tower in which water passes from one container to another in an impromptu waterfall.
- Use an appropriate bubble mixture. Toddlers can feel the bubbles in their hands, ladle them into containers and pour them out again.
- Provide objects that float, such as toy boats and some that sink, unless they are on the boats. Provide words about floating and sinking, but do not expect the children to understand these ideas yet.

Helping out

- Let toddlers help out using water as a cleaning material. They can wipe up the table with a damp cloth or wash up a few spoons and plastic cups. Always thank them for their efforts.
- Show toddlers the source of domestic water from the taps and let them learn about the practical uses of water: drinking, cleaning of all kinds and watering the garden.
- Explain simply what you are doing and whenever possible give the toddlers a safe role in helping you.

Exploring everyday sources of water

- Let toddlers watch the swirl of water as it leaves the sink down the plug hole. Put some floats in the water: they spin in a fascinating way as the water disappears.
- Reassure toddlers who are uneasy about any aspects of water. Some are anxious about plug holes and the flushing of a toilet.
- Take any opportunities to watch the natural flow of water, along the road or gutter and down the drain when it has been raining.

The toddler as traveller

Developmental focus

Toddlers are developing their physical mobility and, within the boundaries for safety, they can walk some of the distance in a local outing or get out of the buggy at an interesting point. Toddlers are curious and ready to learn some names of what they see and hear. They will also point out items of interest to you. Toddlers have much to learn about the world, and objects or events that are very ordinary to you can be novel and intriguing to them.

Toddlers often just enjoy getting out. They do not require expensive trips. Young children are learning so much that is new – their task is often to make sense of it and explore how one experience links with another. Helpful adults look for ways to help toddlers to make those interesting connections. You need a break too, and there are many possibilities even in apparently unpromising areas so long as you think creatively.

Play and learning tips

Check out local possibilities for free or inexpensive outings and share ideas with parents. Keep a file of the details.

Think of child-focused timing. A half-hour trip may get you all no further than round the block. However, the toddlers may have been fascinated to watch two cats playing in a front yard, followed by the exciting sight of a mechanical digger working on the road. To them this is a successful trip.

All these ideas depend, of course, on careful adult supervision that keeps children safe without unnecessarily restricting their enjoyment.

Activities

Build up the ideas

- Have regular outings to the local park (even small areas interest young children), the library, local shops or a market.
- Libraries offer a welcoming environment for browsing. Watch out for special storytelling sessions or music.

Flexible plans

- Pause to look at what interests the children and build in regular local stops for sights that they enjoy and anticipate.
- Tell toddlers about your plans for the trip, for instance, 'We have these letters to post' or 'Let's buy some bread rolls for tea'.
- Nurseries benefit from having a petty cash fund to provide for small purchases which make local trips more special for children.

Look and learn

- Look for safe vantage points to watch transport. Look out for the less usual vehicles like fire engines, police cars and big trucks.
- Observe trains safely from an embankment and wave to the passengers.
- At different seasons there may be plants, flowering shrubs or young birds to visit by looking at local gardens, parks

or recreation grounds.

- After rain, go out to tread in the puddles or make tracks with the buggy wheels. Or you may be lucky enough to see a rainbow. Wrap up warm in cold, snowy weather and go out to make tracks.

Run and look

- Trips to an open space can be fun just to let off energy by running about, jumping, chasing and shouting for fun.
- Even a small park may have some pond life and water birds. A gentle slope can provide enjoyment for climbing up and running down.
- Garden centres have interesting plants but maybe also fountains, mini-waterfalls and garden ornaments. Show toddlers how to look and touch carefully.
- In a more rural environment you may have regular seasonal sights – for example, new lambs or harvesting a crop.

Recognise and recall

- Toddlers enjoy familiar experiences as well as brand new ones. Share their pleasure as they point out their favourite little fountain or the wall where the snails congregate.
- Support toddlers' recognition of a local circuit. For instance, when you approach a familiar landmark from a different direction: 'Look, it's the garden with all the gnomes. We've come from the other side.'

Buying, carrying and collecting

- Show that you trust toddlers and let them hold some things sometimes, perhaps the drinks and snacks for your trip to the park.
- Let toddlers collect items of interest: stones, snail shells and leaves. Wash as necessary and display the collection, or use in creative activities.
- At the post office or bank, they may like to select a few leaflets and forms. Toddlers like this paperwork just because it seems important to adults.
- Involve children in small purchases: the anticipation, selection and payment. Buy stamps or stationery, a banana or a fresh roll to eat now.

Make connections

- Help the children to make links. Perhaps react to excited pointing from toddlers with, 'You're right! We know him. He's our milkman!'
- By about 18 months, toddlers may link local sights with images in books or posters. Be excited if they point out a picture of a squirrel, just like you all saw this morning. Make links yourself in simple conversation with the children, when you share books or look together at posters and wall friezes.

Development within the third year

From their second to their third birthdays, young children change remarkably as they extend their skills, interests and understanding of their personal world. They have a sense of themselves as individuals and can have a positive view of themselves. Already you will see the difference between young children who have been encouraged and those who have experienced far too much criticism or pressure in their lives.

Young children bring their previous experience to bear on the present, and their expectations will shape how they approach play materials or react to new adults. Young children are not egocentric in the way that is often said, namely that they cannot look beyond their own perspective. On the contrary, within this age range, you will see evidence that young children do sometimes consider others and are sometimes aware of what they do not know. It is the adult's responsibility to hold to realistic expectations and to consider the perspective of young children.

Children's physical skills, both large and fine movements, enable them to move around and explore, finding out more about how everyday objects work and experiencing pleasure in their ability to run, jump, climb and play vigorously with their friends. Their skills and understanding of sequence and familiar events can make young children genuinely helpful within the daily routine. Having a trusted part to play supports their confidence and self-esteem.

The ability of young children to use language extends into a broader use of their communication skills as well as an impressive vocabulary. Children's mistakes tend to be logical, based on what they know so far, and are often very sensible guesses beyond that boundary. They show creative uses of language to develop rich pretend play. What they say, the logical mistakes that they often make and the evidence of their imagination remind adults just how much even these young children are already thinking and reasoning.

Physical or learning disabilities will shape the pattern of young children's development, as will persistent ill health. It is the responsibility of caring adults to ensure that disabled children are enabled to play and be part of daily routines, along with appropriate adjustments and realistic expectations in line with the specific disability.

During warm exchanges linked with caring routines, children extend other aspects of their development, including their communication skills and their understanding of how their personal world operates – its patterns and more predictable sequences. An understanding of caring routines is absorbed by young children and then reworked within their pretend play. Then they can use their imagination to take on those responsibilities that would otherwise be unsuitable for them to carry out in real routines.

Contents

82–86 Developing relationships

87–95 Using the senses

96–104 Language and creative development

105–109 Physical development

110–116 Using the environment

developing relationships

Involving young children in physical care

Developmental focus

Food, warmth, suitable physical exercise and sleep are as essential to the young child as to a new-born baby. They need to feel cared for and a sense of love, trust and a feeling of belonging will enable the child to explore and enjoy familiar or new environments. Increasingly, the young child can and wants to take part in her caring routines. There are many opportunities for this, so long as adults take the time. Such involvement promotes children's self-reliance and sense of satisfaction.

Care and learning tips

There will be an element of choice for young children. Perhaps they can feed themselves but today they would like your help. Caring adults adjust to children's moods and preferences when possible.

Children do not learn well if their growing abilities are made into a burden for them. Their confidence and motivation will be dampened if they are told, 'you're nearly three – you ought to be able to...!'

Keep in good communication with parents over the caring routines, including toilet training, feeding and food choices.

Activities

Mealtimes

- Encourage healthy eating by providing suitable snacks for young children. Extend your ideas by talking with parents.
- Allow the children to join in preparation. They can gather the items needed, wash the fruit, or pass the bread to be buttered. Have child-sized spoons or serving bowls so that they can dish up for themselves.
- A variety of items at snack time is important as we all have different tastes, but be sure to encourage children to try everything.
- Present the food in an interesting way, which is enjoyable for all children but may especially encourage less enthusiastic eaters. For example, wrap a little mandarin orange in bright tissue paper, present them in a basket covered in ribbon and get the child to guess what's inside each parcel.
- Ask the children if they would like to help make a menu board or a scrapbook of 'our favourite foods'.

Social mealtimes

- Help to make snack or meal time a pleasant time of company and conversation as well as eating.
- Show a good example yourself of courtesy, sharing and turn taking at snack time. Encourage appropriate language by asking around the table 'Rebecca, would you like one? or 'Dai, could you please pass me...?'
- Draw attention to manners, saying 'Please' and 'Thank you'. But be open minded about ways of expressing appreciation – children can be polite without necessarily using these exact words.

Dressing

- Young children should be encouraged at all times to dress themselves, with appropriate help for awkward bits and fastenings. A child who is tired or ill will need more support.
- Young children should be encouraged to think 'I am hot, I'll take off my jumper', or 'It is cold outside so I need my jacket'. If a child has been outside and stepped in puddles, they can be encouraged to think 'I need dry socks'. If they have forgotten to roll up sleeves or are wet, then they may need to change a piece of clothing.
- The reasons for all of these issues should be pointed out regularly as children get ready to go out, paint or start a vigorous activity. Setting up experiences to highlight these issues helps the children appreciate why they need to think about their clothing!

Does it fit?

- Pick two children very different in size. Allow them to try on each others' jackets and shoes. Introduce words such as 'tight', 'long', 'short', and 'big', but suggest that wearing our own clothes and shoes is still the best idea.
- Gather three or four children into a small area with a basket of clothes that are too small and too big. Offer a challenge to look at the items and guess if they would fit the children. Would they fit you as an adult?
- Gather a small group of children round

a bowl of water. Ask the children to take off their socks. Give them a new pair. Ask them to soak one of the new pair in the water and wring it out. Ask them to put on the dry sock, then the wet sock. Which was easiest to put on? Which feels best?

Keeping clean

■ Gather two or three children round a table with four small bowls with warm water for washing their hands.

■ Ask each child to wash their hands with soap and then to dry them. The adult should do this first, pointing out each finger, the palm, the back of the hand and the wrist while washing. Say a rhyme while you work through the routine.

■ The same kind of experience can be set up to encourage children to wash their faces. Make sure they use their own personal face-cloth to wash behind their ears and necks, on their chins, cheeks and foreheads. Again, a rhyme may help.

■ Bathing dolls is a good way to encourage children to wash and take care of their whole bodies. Ensure you have enough dolls and let children choose a doll to bathe. Give them soap, a towel and a brush. Let them play at bathing the doll freely and then join in, talking through the parts of the doll you are washing to show the children how each part of the body should be washed when in the bath.

Tooth care

■ Help children to learn the habit of brushing teeth after eating – especially after sweet things. However, talk with parents about when children brush their teeth at home – dentists now say that it is possible to over-brush teeth.

■ Brushing teeth can become an enjoyable routine activity. Show children how to put out a little toothpaste, brush all around and rinse. This can be carried out in front of a mirror to encourage them to check that all the teeth are clean.

Rest and quiet time

■ Designate times in the day when children rest together. Children should realise that they can choose to run around, play with resources or rest together.

■ It is often only when children have the option to rest that they do so. Sharing quiet, restful times is a positive experience. Sit with them and keep them company, perhaps with a soft song or story if they wish.

■ Ask the children to sit or lie with their eyes closed. Encourage them to touch their hair, feel their cheeks, gently rub their noses and so on. This type of reflective activity is very popular with adults, and more so with uninhibited children.

Social development – making friends

Developmental focus

Within this age range, young children who have been supported in a sense of their own self-worth are more able to behave in ways that adults recognise as social. However, they are still very young and we owe them the respect of realistic expectations, rather than demanding actions in areas like sharing just because it makes life easier for us as adults. You will help children far more if you assign some thinking time to help them realise just what you are asking if you say, 'Take turns' or 'Think about other people sometimes'.

Young children are more able to recognise and express their feelings but they still have much to learn. They can be overwhelmed by strong emotions, especially since they have few strategies for dealing with upsetting or perplexing social situations.

Young children need help in group life for a wider range of social skills than adults usually recognise. By all means, watch and see if children can manage, but be ready to help where necessary. For example, young children may need your support to join a group that has already begun a play activity. One child may need a sympathetic ear to deal with the distress of being rejected by a group, yet another may need support to make some distance from another child who clings more closely than she wishes.

Play and support tips

- Look carefully at the organisation of your setting or how you arrange children's social life with home-based care. Children cannot get to know each other if they rarely encounter the same children. Very flexible times for a crèche or nursery may suit the adults, but can disrupt the predictability that enables children to make friends.
- Respect children's choices about activities and playmates.
- Show a good example to young children by acknowledging their feelings, listening to them and taking their emotions seriously. You can help and offer comfort as well as share in their delight and fascination.

Getting along

- Watch, listen and let the children show you who are their close friends. Don't tell them that another child is their friend.
- Help young children to relate well together by creating an environment in which they do not have to compete over play materials or adult attention.
- Look carefully at your day and re-organise to avoid times when young children have to wait so long that squabbles are likely or boredom begins.
- Make drinks and nutritious snacks easily available (the self-service snack bar), rather than a long snack time during which toddlers can get cranky. A few children will often make a real choice of 'Let's have our drinks together now'.
- Organise for young children to access the toilet and washing facilities when they need to go and avoid the problems of queuing for toilet time.

Small scale and flexible

- Be flexible in your day and sing with children when they ask for a song or rhyme.
- Sit down with one or two children in the book corner or on floor cushions and share some books that interest them.
- Keep group activities on an intimate

scale for young children so that they can be closely involved and make choices. They cannot cope with big storytime groups or singing sessions.

Early social skills

- Bring one or two young children into a joint activity – for example, helping to tidy up the bricks or doing some basic cooking.
- Thank children for their help or ideas and encourage them to tell others about the activity with 'We found these pieces' or 'Do you want some of our gingerbread?'
- Help children to learn about taking turns by showing how you wait patiently for someone to finish, or ask pleasantly, 'Can I have that when you're finished?'
- Respect children's right to complete what they are doing with a tool or a set of crayons. The answer to another child's, 'Can I have that?' can sometimes be 'No' or 'Soon'.
- Promote the idea of timed turns by using a large sand timer or a mechanical egg timer. Children who experience fairness are more likely to show it in return.
- Set a good example to the children with warm remarks such as, 'I do like that!' or 'Well done, you were so careful with the rabbit'. Listen and you will hear children use similar remarks to each other.

Co-operative games

- Look for activities during which children can work together, with your support. Keep the groups very small, otherwise their interest will fade as they wait.
- Plan a craft activity with easy steps but an impressive end result – perhaps patchwork designs in paper, card or material.
- Simple cooking and food preparation enable young children to take turns and watch each other.
- Indoor or outdoor gardening can draw on young children's physical skills and encourage co-operative activity in digging, planting and watering.
- Use books with repeating phrases for young children to chime in together or to take turns supplying the phrases.
- Make photo books or scrapbooks to record and celebrate joint activities. Parents will be interested, and children will enjoy looking at 'What we all did together'.

Expressing feelings – and respecting other people's

- Listen and avoid telling children what they should or 'ought not' to feel.
- Read stories that explore feelings of individual characters: happiness, excitement, troubles or the feeling of missing someone.
- A puppet or soft toy may also be the main character in a story that you tell which discusses the idea of feelings and raises questions like 'What shall he do?'

using the senses

Looking and learning

Developmental focus

Young children's visual skills should be equivalent to adult abilities. They can see what you see, assuming they don't have visual disabilities, but they cannot make sense of everything yet. Young children are building up their visual experience of the world, and this includes information about qualities of objects such as shapes, size or colour. They need broad opportunities to use their vision in everyday activities, so they will be ready in time to assign words to these qualities. There is no need to rush them with the language for abstract qualities. Young children who are asked too soon about ideas such as colour tend to get confused rather than understand any earlier – and the sense of pressure blocks their learning.

Young children's ability to concentrate will steadily extend when they are encouraged and enabled to use their visual skills carefully and to scan for detail. They enjoy this focussed play and involvement in ordinary daily tasks. Sometimes they just enjoy looking at interesting or new sights. Involved adults can encourage children's willingness to stop and stare and sometimes to be enchanted.

Play and learning tips

Careful looking helps children to remember where materials or tools are kept. Label storage areas in the nursery with simple pictures so children can find things and tidy away by themselves.

Young children build up their visual experience of the world, which includes information about qualities of objects such as shapes, size, relative height or weight and colour.

Talk with parents about the play activities you offer and explain how children are learning. Your conversation can help to calm any sense of pressure parents are feeling. They may be asking themselves questions like, 'When is he going to know his colours!' Display photos of children doing activities on your parents' notice board with a short description of the activities.

Don't feel obliged to have a completed piece of work to show parents, especially if this causes you to put undue pressure on the children. Instead tell parents about activities their child enjoyed that day and share ways to extend the enjoyment at home.

Activities

Busy pictures

- Get books with large pictures of familiar items, such as *What's That?* (Campbell Books, £3.50). Encourage the children to look at the pictures, scanning the details in a relaxed way.
- Ask them to choose their favourite part of the picture and to talk about it if they wish. You can invite them to speak in an open-ended way such as, 'Tell me about the...' or 'What's going on in that corner?'.
- Play search-and-find by asking the children to spot objects, animals or people in a book or poster picture. Begin with easy and familiar items, then try a few more difficult suggestions.
- If children are intrigued by this spotting game, hold up an item and ask the children to find it in the picture. Make some collections of items that link with a given picture.

Copy me

- Stand in front of the children and get them to face you. While demonstrating and naming actions, encourage the children to copy you. For example, touch the floor, jump up and wiggle your nose.
- Get the children to suggest actions and then copy them yourself.
- Develop this idea by introducing the children to 'Simon Says'. Feel free to change it to your own name. And introduce children to action songs where they have to use hand-eye co-ordination, such as 'Head, shoulders, knees and toes' and 'If you're happy and you know it, clap your hands'.

Can you find it?

- Make two sets of ten cards with pictures of everyday items that can be found in the nursery and are easily accessible.
- Place one set of cards in a bright, attractive bag and invite the children to explore its contents.
- Ask questions like 'What have we got here?' to ensure that each child can identify the items on the cards. Then draw their attention to the cards, one at a time, finally asking them to find the real item in the room.
- Talk about the pictures with the children. You might comment on the item itself, the colour, shape or size and where the real item is kept in your room.
- Get the children to place the item and the card next to one another.
- Develop this activity by placing the second set of cards around the room –

on the walls, chairs, table, sink and so on. Hold up a card and ask the children to find its matching partner. Alternatively, shuffle both sets of cards, turn them upside-down on the floor, get each child to pick a card and let the others take turns to find its partner.

- Play 'I spy' with qualities that young children may recognise, for instance, 'I spy with my little eye something that is big and very fluffy'.

Environmental walk

- Take photos of local features outdoors such as the nursery's sign, a local shop and a telephone kiosk.
- Give the children some of the photos, take them on a walk and ask them to look for the items in their photos. Help them as much as they wish.
- Alternatively, use photos of natural items such as fir cones, leaves and twigs.

Touch

Developmental focus

Young children now have a well-developed and sensitive use of touch. This sense is combined with good abilities to look at, grasp and manipulate small and larger objects. They learn from a wide variety of appropriate hands-on experiences of play materials and ordinary objects. Children have some understanding of unpleasant touch, things that are too hot or that hurt or scrape them. They are still learning about common dangers and need adults' patience and guidance to continue to understand so that they can increasingly take good care of themselves.

Friendly touch that acts as contact, communication and comfort is still important, and children may use touch to comfort a friend. They will appreciate your close contact so long as you respect individual preferences of how young children want to be comforted – offer, but don't require cuddles.

Play and learning tips

Children can learn the words to describe how their world feels, but it takes time for them to link a word with the experience of touch. Be patient and ready to repeat what you say in different play activities.

Young children begin to understand complex ideas like 'heavy' or 'light' through hands-on experience, direct touch and feeling the weight of objects.

Activities

Socks off!

- Help children to take off their shoes and socks. Go barefoot as well!
- Sit on the floor with the children and wriggle your toes about.
- Try feeling different objects with just the feet; children can close their eyes and try to guess what the object is if they want. Try a banana, potato or other familiar fruit or vegetables. Feel a book, a teddy, paper tissues or building bricks.
- Try to pick up objects with both feet or the toes. It is not easy, so emphasise the

fun in trying.

- Walk on different-textured surfaces: some lino, a piece of deep pile carpet, some textured wallpaper, a rectangle of foam, the wadding used in quilting, a roll of cotton wool or popper wrap. Introduce words like 'soft', 'rough', 'scratchy' or 'slippery'.
- Put bare feet in the sand pit or a bowl of soft sand. Wriggle your toes in the sand, bury your own or a child's feet and watch the toes break free.

Rub along

- Make rubbings by placing paper against textured surfaces and help children to create an image by rubbing with a wax crayon. Use coins, leaves, paper taped to the bark of a tree or anything suitable with a raised surface. Encourage children to feel the surface before they rub.
- Make a patchwork collage with ready-cut shapes of different material or textured paper and wallpaper. Encourage children to stroke the materials as well as create the patchwork.

Different strokes

- Make a feely book with the children. Have a wide range of materials and sort them out by feel.
- Encourage the children to stroke and touch the materials, and help them with the words to describe what they feel. Soft textures from silk and velvet, flower petals, feathers or cotton wool. Rough textures from velcro, some leaves or a flat scourer. Shiny material from flattened milk bottle tops or lengths of ribbon.
- Some materials may be hard to describe: a bath sponge may be rough or squishy, knitting wool may be fluffy or a bit scratchy.
- Stick the materials into a scrapbook, letting the children make their own choices from the available materials.

Choose some books about touch and the other senses to read to children. One example is the *Touch and Feel* series (Dorling Kindersley, £4.99).

Eyes closed

- Take some familiar objects and toys and put them into a large cloth bag or a cardboard box with a lid.
- Children put a hand into the bag or box, feel for an object and try to guess what it is before bringing it out to see.
- Encourage children to feel carefully before guessing, and help them with the words to describe what they can feel.

- Join in the game yourself and make a couple of deliberate mistakes, especially if the children find it hard to guess.

Heavy and light

- Feel a feather on one hand and a toy car on the other. Show children how to weigh up each side. Try with other objects which vary in weight.
- Have two bags, ideally ones you can see through, and explore how it feels when different objects are put into each bag and they are lifted, one in each hand. Experiment with different amounts of the same objects in each bag, for instance, building bricks or spoons.
- Introduce the words heavy and light and look for opportunities in the day to add to the children's understanding. Perhaps you might say, 'All these books are too heavy for me. Can you help me with some?'

Smelling and learning

Developmental focus

Young children have a well-developed sense of smell and some clear preferences about 'nice' and 'horrid' smells – just like their views on tastes. It is useful for adults to remember that a good sense of smell can help to keep us safe and healthy, for example, by alerting us to food that is going bad or to the danger of fire.

Children can learn more about the range of smells and link appropriate words to the scents when they are offered a rich variety of learning experiences that provide access to new as well as familiar smells. They will extend their language by describing the smells they like and dislike, those they don't mind and those that remind them of certain occasions or places.

Play and learning tips

Continue to talk with parents so that you are aware if children have any allergies or sensitivities. Tell parents about any sensitivities that become evident through activities.

If so, distance the children somewhat from the toiletries or perfumes. You can avoid direct contact by putting the substance on to small sticky-backed address labels – or just ensure that the children smell without touching.

Don't expect too much in terms of language from children to talk about smells – adults often do not have a rich vocabulary for describing or distinguishing scents, pleasant or otherwise.

Share with parents how you alert children to everyday smells and invite them to enjoy this experience with their children at home. Parents might like to share the different smells around the home, such as flowers in a vase, cooking or fresh food, washing from the tumble dryer or toiletries in the bathroom.

Spread out the suggested activities; there is no intention that you blast children with smells! Take your time and help them to notice and comment.

Activities

Cooking smells

■ Alert children to the smells of food and cooking. Point out the smells of ingredients when you do simple cooking with children.

■ You can place jelly in warm water, watch it melt and smell it. Include a variety of essences in baking activities.

■ Suggest that when cooking at home, parents allow their child to smell the rich and varied scents of the food they use, as well as any herbs, spices or sauces that are added to flavour the foods.

Bathroom and washing smells

■ Have pleasant-smelling soaps to encourage the children to wash their hands. Alert them to the scent of other toiletries, either that you have in the nursery bathroom or that you wear.

■ Young children may start to recognise familiar toiletries such as perfume, deodorant, bubble bath, shaving foam, soap, toothpaste or aftershave. Make the links with parents to scents in the home.

■ In the nursery and through links to children's homes, draw children's attention to the scents of washing powder, fabric conditioner and washing-up liquid. Use any natural opportunities to confirm that some cleaning substances are not for children, only for adults to use.

■ Put different scents, for example, peppermint or lemon essence, soap flakes or bubble bath, into play dough and water.

Perfumed pictures

■ Collect scented crayons, pens or pencils, paper, ordinary crayons and a brightly-coloured bag.

■ Give each child a blank sheet of paper and encourage her to use ordinary crayons to make marks on the paper. Invite children to smell the picture.

■ Now put the scented crayons in the bag, ask what they think you have in it, and suggest that it is something that can make their pictures have a scent.

■ Ask each child to take out one of the crayons. In a low voice stress how special they are. Invite them to smell one of the special crayons, then an ordinary one, and ask, 'Are they different?'.

■ Ask children to use the special crayons to draw a picture and then smell it.

■ If children are interested, extend this activity by using each crayon separately. Invite the children to smell each colour once and guess the smell.

Smelly soaps

■ Place four to six bars of fruit-scented soap, wrapped in some netting, inside a large, decorative bag. Ask the children to take them out one at a time and invite them to identify the smell. Bear in mind that some scented soaps are closer to their supposed smell than others.

■ Encourage them to pass the soap on to the next child and to describe it if they wish, by shape, colour, smell or any other quality.

■ Ask children for their opinions – do they like the scent or not, or which is their favourite?

■ Cover the soap with cotton, then ask the children to identify just by smell, having taken away the colour that sometimes gives the clue.

- Allow the children to wash their hands with their favourite bar.

What's that smell?

- Place a variety of items, such as grated chocolate, orange peel, sliced banana, sherbet, peppermint cream, grated cheese and jelly cubes into small bowls or containers.
- Ask the children to take time to smell each one. Then blindfold one child, offer her an item and invite her to guess which it is. Repeat with the other children.
- While the children are blindfolded, introduce a new item to challenge their smelling skills – tell them 'This is a new smell'.
- They can taste some items after they have identified them.

Making perfume

- For this activity, you will need a variety of flowers, small containers, a bottle of liquid perfume made from flowers and already prepared by an adult. Essential oil or rosewater will enhance the perfume, but check for any allergies and ensure undiluted oil doesn't touch the children's skin. You also need an orange, a variety of perfumes and aftershaves, and a mortar and pestle.
- Place a small container in front of each child and give him one or two flowers. Suggest that he removes the petals and places them in the containers.
- Let children smell the bottle of perfume and aftershave. Then offer the liquid perfume and invite children to guess how they think the liquid appeared.
- To help them understand, crush some of the petals using a mortar and pestle and squeeze an orange. Explain there are only tiny amounts of liquid in the flowers and that we add water to make the perfume.
- Ask them to help crush the petals, and add some water. Then invite them to rub scented water or petals onto their wrists.

Hearing and listening

Developmental focus

By this age, young children are able to name many sounds and match them to their source. Children can be encouraged to develop their powers of auditory discrimination when you incorporate sound into everyday activities in the nursery, and you alert children to sounds within the daily routine. Young children's ability to concentrate is a combination of looking and listening. So activities that help them to listen and make sound deliberately can support their growing ability to focus.

Young children are interested in a range of activities that involve rhythm, basic movement and exploration of beat. They can learn how to tune into sounds as well as experience a sense of achievement by making the kinds of sounds and patterns that they want to create for themselves.

Use of percussion instruments can

combine sound and feel since they produce vibrations that children can experience as well as creating the actual sounds.

Play and learning tips

Young children are interested in a range of activities that involve rhythm, basic movement and exploration of beat.

Set a good example to young children by listening yourself and following their suggestion to hear an interesting or intriguing sound.

Record the children regularly and let them listen to themselves. They will initially doubt that it is indeed their own voice.

Ensure that children have a quiet environment sometimes - as well as a lively environment.

Make sure that you are close to children so that they can hear you clearly. Get their attention first and resist shouting across a room. When you give directions, wait for children to follow them and then repeat if you need.

Get to know individual children - some are uneasy in noisy environments and will want peaceful times or quiet corners.

Activities

Hearing the sounds

- Use an instrument or a bell as a listening focus to call children's attention or to signal part of the routine - such as tidying up or lunchtime.
- Play a range of games to identify recognisable sounds, including sound lotto.
- Make and use a variety of instruments with the children.
- Repeat a rhyme several times, then leave out the rhyming word and let the children fill in the missing word.

Getting it on tape

- Show children a microphone and tape recorder and tell them that you will record their voices.
- Ask the children to say a rhyme, one at a time or in pairs. Record the rhyme and play it back.
- Put in a tape of previously recorded sounds around the home, such as a running tap, ringing telephone or door bell, flushing toilet, laughing children, car starting or a beeping car horn.
- Ask the children what they hear and then ask if they would like to make a tape. Take them outside to identify noises they want to tape, such as children playing, dogs barking, a 'green man' beeping or a fire engine siren.
- Let each child record a sound then return to a quiet area to listen to the tape.
- As a follow-up, you could record the children talking or singing, and let them record each other.

Noisy trays

- Fill trays with a large amount of items, such as pasta, rice, cotton wool balls, marbles and tin foil. Watch that the children do not put small items into their noses or mouths.

■ Place the trays on the floor and give each child a bean bag. Ask them to drop the bean bag on to the tray and then to describe the noise.
■ Let them play with the bean bags and trays as they wish. You could suggest that they use their hands and feet to make a noise on the tray.
■ As a follow up, place the trays in an open box, so the children can throw the bean bags into them. Before they throw the bags, ask them, 'Will it be noisy? What do you think?'.

Strumming

■ Let the children look at a guitar and ask them what they think will happen if you touch the strings. Some children may recognise the instrument if someone at home plays the guitar.
■ Let them touch the strings. Strum and pick the strings, making notes yourself and then allow the children to experiment.
■ Repeat the experience with a violin or other stringed instrument.
■ Talk about the hole in each instrument. Then offer the tissue boxes and elastic bands, and ask if they can suggest a way to make their own guitars.
■ Let the children attempt to do this, giving help when asked.
■ Have a little concert if the children would like to.

Telephone conversations

■ Collect some old telephones or realistic toy telephones. Record a variety of comments or questions to stimulate responses on a telephone answering machine.
■ Let the children play with the old telephones and then explain that you are going to set up an answering machine.
■ Let the children press play on the machine and answer questions during a gap, such as 'How are you today?', 'What did you do last night?'.

When to worry

Similar issues and concerns still apply as were raised on page 59. Keep the communication open with parents and have a full conversation with families whose disabled child joins your setting.

Encourage parents to obtain medical checks where appropriate since difficulties in vision or hearing, however slight, will complicate the learning task for young children and delay them from receiving appropriate help.

language and creative development

Early communication

Developmental focus

Young children now use many more words and combine them into meaningful and original phrases and then short sentences. Their mistakes in word combinations or basic grammar are usually logical. By the end of the year, children use their language in different ways, such as asking questions and telling you about events. They work to express feelings or simple ideas. Some children will be learning two languages and can successfully become bilingual speakers.

Children's understanding of what is said to them has expanded tremendously. Also they will have learned a range of strategies for showing that they do not understand you or need more information. Depending on their experience, young children can be learning the social skills of communication – the skills of listening and trying not to interrupt.

Familiar carers should understand most of what children say and it would be a source of concern if a three-year-old were incomprehensible to a parent or familiar carer. In the same way, children should show that they understand simple language from familiar adults and children. They still use all the clues of the situation and predictable routines, but children should now understand the words as well.

Play and learning tips

Individual conversations are very important for young children, and how you behave sets a good example – showing interest, listening and waiting rather than interrupting are all important for children to see. The key is to talk with children, not at them, and to listen as much as you talk.

Sometimes start the conversation, but make sure that you also follow the children's lead, listening to what interests them, and the questions they want to ask you.

Make sure that you sometimes ask children questions when you do not know the answer, so they can have the pleasure of telling and explaining.

Do some 'research' by looking at a child's favourite book or television programme so you understand what he wants to share with you.

Talk with parents so you can know who are the potentially bilingual children in your setting. Speak the language in which you are most fluent, but it would be friendly to learn some words in the child's home language as well.

Activities

Will you help?

- Children like to be involved in the daily routine; it makes them feel valued and trusted. There will be many opportunities for them to practise their understanding and their own words.
- Ask children to take simple messages to another adult or child, perhaps initially just across the room. Help them if they forget or get muddled. Always thank them for their help.
- Ask children for their opinion when choices, such as how best to display their models, can be made.
- If a small group of children come up with several possibilities, then involve them in the plan to put the choices in order, for instance, the stories they would like to be read this afternoon. 'So, first we'll have... then we'll...'.
- Involve them in tasks that need some thought or planning. It might be: 'I can't find the thick paper. Where do you think we put that away?' or 'Let's go to the baker's this afternoon. What shall we buy for a treat for tea?'. 'What will we need to take with us on the trip?'.
- When children have a rich range of experiences, they will rework them in their pretend play.

Are you feeling...?

- Children may have the words for many familiar objects, people and actions, but expressing feelings is more complex. Without telling children what they feel, help them to put some possible words to their emotions.
- Watch them and listen to what they say, so that your suggestions can be sensible as well as tentative.
- It might be, 'Harry, you look a bit sad. Are you sad about something?' or 'Angie, are you cross about the collage? I know, it's very annoying when you've worked hard and things won't go right.'

I wonder what...?

- Encourage children to use their words to speculate and wonder.
- With a familiar or a new book, ask the children, before you turn the page, 'Ooh, what's going to happen now?' or 'How will he get out of this mess?'
- Use daily opportunities to involve children in considering a range of possibilities, like, 'Our tomato plants are so tall they keep falling over. What could we do to help them stay up?' or 'I wonder what'll happen when we add the water to this mixture.'

Do you remember when...?

- Young children love to reminisce about shared past experiences. It may be something exciting, puzzling or just a happy time.
- It can be fun to relive experiences through words – or maybe photographs as well.
- Follow children's lead when they want to talk about the fire engine you all saw yesterday or the dead baby bird that you buried in the garden last week.
- Share your memories as appropriate. Perhaps smile and say, 'I was remembering when I stepped in that big puddle and you all laughed so hard.'

Having a good natter

- Children will enjoy talking with each other. Value their conversations, listen in sometimes and avoid interrupting them.
- Look to create quiet areas inside and in the garden where friends, or you and the children, can simply sit and chat.

The young child as artist

Developmental focus

Young children who are given a range of materials are fascinated by their ability to create beautiful images, unusual designs and new textures. At this age, children are unlikely to set out with the intention of drawing anything specific, although three-year-olds may start to tell you that their painting is of a person or object.

Creative activities give children pleasure and satisfaction and provide a positive focus for their physical skills and visual abilities. They will still enjoying painting with hands and fingers, but can also manage chunky brushes and other tools. Young children benefit from having a range of colours and textures from which to choose. They will also benefit from the chance to experiment with their own ideas – rather than simply copying examples made by adults.

Children's personal and emotional development is supported when you are appreciative of their efforts and what they finally produce. Respect what they say the drawing or model represents, or the fact that it is not in their view anything in particular.

Play and learning tips

Always display children's work attractively and do not demand unrealistic artistic standards. Children will be really disappointed if their work is not displayed with everyone else's.

Where possible, gather examples of children's work or photos in their personal portfolio for them to keep.

Avoid asking children the direct question of 'What is it?'. They will tell you if their creation needs a name. You can comment on the colours, swirly textures or dramatic shapes.

Some paint is very hard to get off clothes, so cover children well and pass on any tips to parents about how best to wash out some colours. If PVA glue gets on woollen clothes, place them in the freezer overnight and pick it off the next day.

Activities

Using the tools

- Experiment to find the size of brush or other tools that individual children can best manage.
- Let two-year-olds practise using scissors. They will be safe if you remain close and you can then help them. Children often appreciate someone holding the paper firmly while they cut. Allow the children to snip thin, pre-cut lengths of paper.

So many ways to paint!

- Sit one or two children down at a wipeable table with two or three colours of paint. Show them the paint and talk about the colours. Shake a tin of shaving foam and squirt a pile in front of each child. Encourage the children to choose a colour of paint to mix with the foam. While they experiment with mixing, they can 'paint' the table, drawing a pattern with their fingers. The children could take a print of any pattern they make.
- Give children buckets of water and large paintbrushes and allow them to paint an outdoor wall.
- Children enjoy creating pictures using a range of sticky-backed shapes.
- Add a range of smells to paint in order to vary the experience. Try adding vanilla or peppermint essence, cinnamon, cloves or lemon juice.
- Clean a selection of roller-ball deodorant bottles before giving them to the children. If they are screwtop, fill with poster paint; if not, get children to dip them in a tray of paint and then make marks on paper.
- Roll out a large length of plain wallpaper. Pour a selection of colours of paint into trays. Have a small bowl of tea bags that the children can dip into and absorb a fair amount of the paint, and then get them to drop the tea bags, splashing them onto the wallpaper.
- Mix icing sugar with water to form a syrup-like consistency. Get the children to use a thick brush to cover a sheet of paper with the mixture and then ask them to dip straws into small pots of paint or food colouring and create patterns. Let the designs dry.

Home-made glue

- Make paste from one cupful of flour and a pinch of salt, then add water until it has a gooey consistency.
- Add a little food colouring to the glue and let the children spread it onto large

sheets of paper.

- Then let the children sprinkle shredded paper, sequins or glitter on to the glued sheet of paper.

Printing

- Printing allows children to create attractive and interesting patterns quickly and easily. You can make paint thicker by adding a little flour. Encourage children to experiment with a range of printing techniques.
- Natural items can be used, such as shells, leaves, flowers, sliced fruit – oranges, apples, starfruit, and vegetables – peppers, carrots and onions.
- Or try combs, corrugated card, cotton reels, sponges, keys, jigsaw pieces and toothbrushes.
- Halve potatoes and then cut shapes into them. Show the children how to paint and print with them.
- For screen printing, roll a sponge over a doily or other patterned item.
- Fold some paper in half and open it up again. Dip some string into the paint, making sure it all gets covered. Put the string on to one half of the paper and fold the other side of the paper on top of it. Press down hard all over, then open. For a different effect, put something heavy, like a book on top of the folded piece of paper and slowly pull out the string.

Play dough

- Children enjoy holding soft, pliable materials like clay and dough in their hands. They can squeeze it to make shapes, or they can simply pull, poke, roll, twist and knead it.
- There is a range of recipes for play dough, and you can vary the experience for children by adding textures, colours and smells (see fingerpainting for toddlers on page 65).
- Provide the children with different items to use with the play dough. For example, biscuit cutters, rolling pins, potato mashers, garlic press, scissors, old cotton reels, tractors and cars to make wheel prints.

Salt dough models

- Make models with the children using this recipe. Get 200g salt, 200g plain flour and 125ml water. Mix the flour and salt in a large bowl. Add water that is at room temperature, and mix. Knead into a smooth, elastic dough.
- Let children shape the dough as they wish, and then slowly bake their creations in a preheated oven at 120°C for three to

four hours.

- Help the children to paint or varnish the models when cool.

Papier-mâché

- Ask any parents who work in an office if they can donate the paper from their shredder to the nursery.
- Soak it in water overnight, squeeze out the surplus water and add wallpaper paste (ensure it does not contain fungicide).

Let children shape the material as they wish, then let it dry out.

Enjoying and making music

Developmental focus

Young children can enjoy making and listening to music, but adults need to ensure that musical activities are a pleasure and not a source of pressure to perform - nor to learn specific instruments at a very young age.

Children practise their physical skills and use their communication in music-making, singing and listening. They will move to rhythms, make sounds with toys and instruments, sing, chant and listen to a variety of forms of music. Singing with children is an effective way to support their language skills and vocabulary. Young children often sing spontaneously as they go about their day-to-day play activities. They enjoy experimenting with instruments and the sounds they create. Live music and singing performances are a source of interest for many children, either to perform themselves or listen and watch others.

Play and learning tips

Never insist that young children perform in front of a group. Invite everyone to do this as individuals, but neither press, nor label the less enthusiastic ones as 'shy'. Let them go public in their own time.

Children's horizons can be broadened if you invite parents or other local people who sing or play instruments to come and share their talents in the nursery.

Starting to play a tape or a CD is a useful way to let children know it is time to tidy up or to gather for storytime if they wish.

Activities

Music corner

- Set up an area in the nursery where children can experiment with different instruments.
- Place the instruments in storage boxes where the children can easily access them. Label the boxes with pictures of the instruments so that they can return them to the correct box.
- Allow the children to experiment with them freely.
- Sometimes tape the sounds the children create and play them back. Invite the children to point to the instruments as they hear them being played on the tape.

Old Macdonald's band

- After the children have been introduced

to a wide range of musical instruments and are familiar with their names, you can adapt the popular 'Old Macdonald had a farm' to 'Old Macdonald had a band'. In that band he had some: bagpipes, drums, bells, guitars, tambourines, triangles, violins, recorders and so on. Get the children to mime the actions of playing the instrument, or to make the appropriate sound while singing the song.

Matching shakers

- Collect containers such as film roll canisters or margarine tubs.
- Fill two of each container with materials that create a noise when shaken, for example, rice, sand, glitter and pennies.
- Use these as percussion instruments to accompany songs.

Sound story

- When children become familiar with songs and stories, they can be made more interactive by adding sounds.
- For example, for 'Goldilocks and the Three Bears', one child can be given wooden blocks or a pair of shoes to tap on the floor for Goldilocks' feet. An empty bowl and spoon can be used for testing the porridge. When the beds are being tried, one child could pat a pillow or cushion. When the bears come back, three instruments can be used to represent each of the bears, for example, a drum for daddy bear, a tambourine for mummy and maracas for baby bear.
- Breaking the story into parts and listening to the sounds helps develop their ability to listen, as well as encouraging an awareness of the sounds instruments make.

Flying scarves

- Collect old silk or cotton neck scarves in the nursery (ask parents to donate or buy them from second-hand shops).
- Select a piece of taped music and take the children to a large, open space indoors or outdoors.
- Play the music and get the children to dance to the music with a scarf in each hand.
- Give children instructions. For example, wave your scarves up in the air, wave them really quickly, wave them behind your back. Demonstrate each action as you go.

Personal song book

- Gather a repertoire of songs and rhymes. These develop children's awareness of the sounds that make up the beginnings and ends of words in the language, and so helps early literacy.
- Gather songs and rhymes to help early numeracy skills. For example, 'Five little speckled frogs' and 'Ten green bottles'.
- Make routines more interesting by making up songs to go along with the actions, for example, 'This is the way we wash our hands' or 'This is the way we brush our teeth' to the tune of 'Here we go round the mulberry bush'.

Tell me a story

Developmental focus

Stories are an important part of the day for young children because listening to different kinds of story supports their all-round development. Stories can be enjoyed through books read out loud by an adult, but stories are also enjoyed through oral story-telling without a book, songs, poems and rhymes.

Telling or reading a story to this age group should still be a personal time. Children approaching three years are more able to manage a group storytime, but they will continue to enjoy and really need the close attention of being with an adult and only one or two other children. When a child says spontaneously, 'Tell me a story!' you are given the opportunity to return to her favourites, and show pleasure at her choices. Your positive reaction supports her emotional development and sense of self-esteem.

Good stories for young children unfold with a recognisable rhythm, and this experience helps children to tune into sounds and sound patterns as they occur in everyday speech. This phonemic awareness, which needs to be offered within the shared activity and without any pressure on the child, will help them a great deal when they are finally ready to read.

Repetition within a story and having favourite stories told many times helps children to anticipate, recall and join in as they wish. This experience supports their language and thinking skills. An early pleasure in books, both the stories and the illustrations, is an invaluable support to the development of children's literacy. For young children, enjoying the story is just as important as gaining an awareness of how books and print work.

Play and learning tips

By this age, children are ready for longer stories – but do not remove the 'baby books' just yet. Slightly older children often still love to have stories they first encountered as toddlers re-told over and over again.

Listen in and encourage children. They will be able to re-tell some stories to themselves as they turn the pages of the book. They may even tell the story to a younger child in the nursery or a sibling at home.

Be ready to repeat favourite stories. By all means, introduce new books and take the children to the local library to explore their own new choices. It is best to mix old favourites with some new stories.

Activities

Once upon a time...

- Practise your story-telling skills – good stories do not only come from books.
- Stretch your range by learning different traditional tales from parents or grandparents and consulting books that draw on a variety of story-telling traditions from different cultures.
- Get to know children's favourite stories

well enough that you can tell them by heart. Be expansive with your gestures and facial expressions in order to conjure up the scene.

■ Story-telling comes in very handy if you and the children are waiting for something for a long time, for example, an appointment or the arrival of a train or bus.

Personal stories

■ Telling a story requires a narrative – a sequence of linked events. Narrative appears in books, as well as in children's recollection of personal or shared experiences.

■ Follow the children's lead if they ask you to re-tell their story with, 'Talk about the big puddle' or 'Say the pussy cat story'.

■ Involve the children with, 'Once upon a time, Jane went to the market with...' (invite the names of the children), followed by 'And then what happened was...' and 'But what did we see then? It was...'.

■ Re-tell favourite shared experiences in a very similar format each time, so that children can join in easily if they want.

■ If children become fond of a bird or animal that visits your setting, make up some stories about what 'Robbie Robin' or 'Henrietta Hedgehog' does when you do not see them.

Making storybooks

■ Make the book of children's personal stories. Create a simple scrapbook or a sequence of photos in a self-seal album.

■ Be ready to tell the story to the children or help them as they tell parts of what happened, pointing to the illustrations.

■ See if the children want to illustrate your stories of the nursery hamster or a wild creature that visits the nursery.

Different story-tellers

■ Support a tale or a story poem with a puppet or suitable soft toy. Be creative in how you share the story with your fellow story-teller.

■ Perhaps teddy or the hand puppet tells the story. Or you may be the story-teller, with two finger puppets commenting on, interrupting or even arguing over the events.

■ Stories linked with television may have the main characters available as soft toys or puppets. Children may like to tell part of a recent episode through the toy. Many children watch a lot of television and this activity helps them make connections in an active story-telling role.

Story poems and rhymes

■ Good stories in the oral tradition (for adults as well as children) are often close to being poems.

■ Look for some story poems, for instance, modern writers such as Michael Rosen, or examples from previous generations, such as A.A. Milne.

■ Tell the story poems with expression – the rhythm helps children to chime in, especially with repeating phrases. Add some suitable gestures and children will join in those as well.

■ Children enjoy it when you pause before a key phrase or gesture and then deliver it, often with their loud addition.

physical development

On the move

Developmental focus

Young children are now well co-ordinated and physically strong compared with babies. They are able to catch balls that are thrown directly into their arms, to stand on one foot, to stand and walk on tiptoe and to make other, more controlled movements. Children love practising and applying their skills in play and lively games. They also need and enjoy space and playmates just for running about and letting off steam. The children's physical skills, and the importance of healthful exercise, can all be incorporated into your plans for the days, both with and without additional equipment.

Some young children are more confident than others. Careful support can encourage less bold children to extend their skills at their own pace. Young children need a safe enough environment and adults who help to keep them from harm. However, they also need challenge and opportunities to begin to assess for themselves the element of risk in each activity: 'how high do I go?' or 'how do we stop banging into each other?'.

Play and learning tips

Create an area for large-scale construction, climbing, dancing and movement. Children appreciate space where they move around without worrying about banging into people or furniture.

Ensure that you have equipment that is suitable for children with disabilities. Many nurseries have discovered that equipment designed initially for disabled children, like wedges and ball pools, is equally enjoyed by children without any physical or health disability. The equipment is truly inclusive.

Provide climbing equipment and wheeled vehicles and barrows to allow young children to exercise their larger muscles.

Make sure you use an outdoor play area to the full, with appropriate materials to hand such as umbrellas, wellingtons, scarves and gloves in case of bad weather.

Activities

Get moving

- To make your programme more varied, carry out some of the activities outdoors or use music to stimulate the children's interest.
- Encourage the children to start playing movement games, such as tag, musical statues and ring around the roses.
- Children of this age can be introduced to skipping ropes, bean bags and hoops to encourage physical activity.

Obstacle course

- Create an obstacle course. You could include: an old box to climb through, large pillows to climb over, a fabric tunnel to crawl through, hoops to step through, a board to walk across, cones to run in and out of and a short, low slide with a mat or ring at the bottom and balls to roll.
- Invite the children to help build and then enjoy the course.

Musical moves

- Put on a tape or CD with lively, happy music. Move in different ways and encourage the children to copy you.
- Try some of these movements: waving your arms, nodding your head, swaying back and forth, stamping your feet, rocking from side to side, shaking your hands and clapping your hands.
- Follow some of the children's own ideas for movements.

Triangle games

- Sit on the floor with a child and face each other in a straddle position, or as close as you can get, and hold hands.
- Lean forwards and encourage the child to lean back, then alternate.
- Sing a variety of songs while doing this – for example, 'Row, row, row your boat' or 'See-saw, Margery Daw'.

Hunt the bear

- Read *We're Going on a Bear Hunt* by Michael Rosen and Helen Oxenbury (Walker Books, £4.50), or tell the story to the children so they become familiar with it.
- Vary the story according to the children's interests, for example, swimming across the ocean, riding a horse, walking a dog or roller-skating.
- Encourage the children to use their bodies to represent the actions in the storm. Then add your own variations – for example, a jellyfish in the ocean, a monster in a loch, a crocodile in the mud or an eagle in the sky.

Controlling movements

- Encourage the children to become more deliberate and controlled in their large movements. Show them movements and invite them to copy.

- They could jump up and down and land with their feet together and then apart, or land with their left foot forward, then land with their right foot forward.
- Stand facing a child, holding each other's hands, and then slowly lean to one side, lifting the other leg off the ground. Then swap legs.

Using fine motor skills

Developmental focus

Young children now have an impressive array of fine physical skills, and these support them in their wish to become more independent in daily life. For example, young children will be able to manage many of the tasks involved in feeding themselves and drinking. They will be able to use everyday implements like a spoon, or to eat fairly neatly with their fingers. Around familiar settings, they will be able to turn a knob to open a door, unscrew lids or pull out the container they want for their play. They are far more able now to manage fine movements required in order to turn the pages of a book one at a time, and to handle the fastenings and more tricky parts of dressing and undressing themselves.

The development of fine motor skills takes time and practice. Adults at home or in the nursery owe children patience and understanding as two- and three-year-olds attempt to master the skills that depend on finger and thumb co-ordination, and linking vision with physical skills and planning.

Play and learning tips

Build up children's confidence by introducing them to more challenging play materials as they are ready. For example, this age range will be more able to handle jigsaws with several pieces and smaller construction materials.

Support children's confidence by offering help as they wish and creating enough of a challenge and novelty to interest, but not daunt children.

Offer extra support and equipment as appropriate to disabled children, but watch any unhelpful tendency for adults to push 'help' when the child does not want it. Keep in mind that disabled children will want to apply and extend their skills just like their friends.

Offer a wide range of materials for pretend play – then children can practise skills on activities that you might not allow them to do for real.

Place an old typewriter or computer keyboard in the role-play corner for the children to 'type' on. Look for other possibilities of real objects with which children can safely play.

Activities

Doing it myself

- To help the development of children's fine motor skills and aid their growing independence, provide cups and eating utensils that are small enough to fit in their hands.

■ Place tissues and paper towels where children can reach them easily. Place coat hooks at the children's height; provide individually-marked toothbrushes for each child, and place them in an accessible location.

■ Encourage children to hang up their own paintings to dry on a string 'clothesline' using clothes pegs.

Rip it up!

■ Allow children the opportunity to rip up old wrapping paper, foil, magazines, newspapers and wallpaper samples. Look for ways that children can use the ripped material if possible – perhaps for collage.

■ Outdoors, they can use dry leaves that shred easily.

■ Emphasise that this is a fun activity and that they shouldn't tear up things unless told to do so by an adult. Children should learn that some activities are only okay if an adult has given them permission to do so.

Fill it up!

■ Get an empty wine box carrier that has separate compartments. Give the children empty plastic water bottles. Encourage them to fill up the box by placing an empty bottle in each compartment.

■ When the children have mastered this task with empty bottles, fill the bottles up with coloured water (tap water and food colouring) and let them continue with the task in hand.

■ In the bath or beside a bowl of water, give the children some empty bottles. Encourage them to unscrew the tops and use the lids as pouring vessels to fill the bottles.

Vegetable and fruit lift

■ Give each child two plates. On one, place a grape, a slice of carrot, a long slice of cucumber, a Smartie and a cube jelly.

■ Encourage them to move each item using their mouths, teeth and lips, from one plate to the next. Then allow them to eat the items!

Finger play

■ Young children thoroughly enjoy finger play using simple rhymes.

■ Try 'Hickory Dickory Dock' with words and gestures. 'Hickory, dickory, dock! (rest elbow in the palm of the other hand and swing upraised arm back and forth), the mouse ran up the clock; (creep the fingers up the arm to the palm of the other hand), the clock struck one (clap hands), the mouse ran down (creep fingers down the elbow). Hickory, dickory, dock! (swing arms as before).'

■ Gather a repertoire of finger play and gesture rhymes. Ask parents for any ideas to extend your selection.

Textured scribbles

■ Give the children who are fairly confident in using crayons a new experience by taping sandpaper, a piece of plastic netting, a square of carpet or corrugated card to a tabletop.

■ Tape large sheets of newsprint or wallpaper on top, and allow the children to scribble. This will encourage them to hold their crayons firmly.

Mosaic

■ Collect pencil sharpenings, sequins, petals, small pieces of wool and string.

■ Encourage the children to arrange them on to a card or box. Suggest that they may want to glue them on to make a gift.

Practice for little fingers

■ Encourage children to practise the skills necessary to dress themselves by attaching different fasteners to a large square of plywood.

■ You could nail or staple the following types of fastenings – Velcro, button, zips, poppers, toggles and shoelaces. Ensure the nails and staples are covered to prevent injury.

■ A similar activity board can be made using a variety of knobs, handles and locks. Secure these to the plywood and let the children experiment with them.

Snack time

■ Encourage children, as far as possible, to select and prepare their own snacks.

■ Let them spread their own toast or crackers with margarine or cheese.

■ Allow them to peel their own fruit and pour milk or juice from a jug into their own cups.

■ Let them mop up any spills.

using the environment

Getting outside

Developmental focus

Most children are now confidently mobile to reach whatever part of your garden or yard they wish to explore. They still have a limited grasp of risk and outdoor hygiene. So, your role is to continue to offer friendly supervision and keep a close eye on hand washing after some activities - especially any kind of gardening.

The children are ready and keen to learn more words about what they see and do in the garden, to talk about the activities and to reminisce with you later about enjoyable sights and games. The outdoors may be some children's favourite place to look, listen and use their senses. Young children who enjoy the outdoors will be ready to extend their interests with simple, illustrated reference books - they may then spot what they see in a favourite picture book out in the garden.

Play and learning tips

Outdoor activities support children's knowledge of the world, as well as their motivation to discover more. Share their interests, talk and listen and you will help the children to make vital connections within their daily experience.

Be creative - even a small outdoor space can be of interest to children. Talk with parents and explain how you use the outdoors with the children. Family members may have plant cuttings to give you or time to help with reorganising an outdoor space.

Activities

Green fingers

- Do some planting with the children. They can learn about digging or making a small hole and patting down the plant, bulb or seedling.
- If you have limited growing space, then invest in pots, window boxes or grow bags. Using only clean earth or compost will be especially important if cats or dogs get into your garden, or your area has a high tetanus risk.

■ Provide some small watering cans for children to sprinkle their plants or any other parts of the garden, especially during hot spells.

■ Talk with the children about the plants, flowers and grasses. Share their delight as the shoots start to push through the earth. Plant some vegetables or fruit that can be eaten later in the year.

Taking the indoors outside

■ In better weather, take play materials outside, such as the sand and water tray, painting easels or construction materials, and put them on an outdoor table.

■ Set up an outdoor activity of washing the dolls' clothes or other small play materials. Talk about what you are doing and introduce relevant words like 'wet' and 'dry'.

■ Have drinks or snacks outside and let the children enjoy the experience of eating al fresco in their own 'café'. Perhaps one or two would like to 'take the orders' and then serve the 'customers'.

Pavement art

■ If you have a paved area, you can encourage the children to be pavement artists with plenty of coloured chalks.

■ Mark out a roadway for the children's play with small cars, or for a route they follow on their trikes and push or pull along vehicles.

■ Chalk some large shapes with the children and play stepping into and out, or walking along a wide line.

■ Make an area of the yard damp with water and let the children make wet footprints out and away over the dry area.

■ Experiment with painting with water on a dry surface using big brushes. On a hot day, watch together, perhaps counting the seconds for how long it takes for their drawings to dry and vanish.

Physical fun

■ Young children still like '1,2,3–go', hide-and-seek and run-and-chase. They also like simple outdoor music and movement, or following you around the garden in a weaving 'snake' line.

■ Use the garden for an obstacle course and let children experience with their entire bodies what it means to go under, round, through and over the top of the items of equipment you have used.

Let's pretend

■ Young children love large boxes, and love imagining them as cars, boats, fire engines as well as homes or castles.

■ Build hideaways and camps with the children by throwing a large sheet or blanket over the climbing frame, or putting up a small tent in the garden. Let them bring out a selection of pretend play material from the home corner to equip their den.

■ Take some photos of the activities so that you can all enjoy them later as you remember together.

Let's do weather

■ Keep track of the weather each day. Let the children look carefully out of the window or go out into the garden. Find the right picture and get a written label to fix onto your weather board. Introduce them to words about warm, cold or windy and to talking about sunshine, rain or clouds.

- Wrap children up warmly to enjoy a fall of snow in the garden. Let them enjoy the delight of making footsteps in the fresh snow. Look for bird or animal tracks.
- Watch the rain from indoors and when it has stopped, go outside and explore where the water has gathered, where it goes down the drains and how much it has filled up any containers in the garden.

Garden creatures

- Help children to learn the names of the creatures they see in the garden: squirrels, spiders, butterflies and perhaps a toad if you are lucky.
- Build children's general knowledge by looking with them for pictures of similar creatures, or flowers and trees in their books.
- Take photographs of the wildlife and plants at different seasons. Make a photo book and help children recall what you all saw or their earlier gardening exploits.

Bringing the outdoors inside

- Try some indoor gardening: sprouting carrot or pineapple tops on a window shelf or some herbs.
- Grow mustard and cress on damp blotting paper or cotton and eat some when it is ready. Be aware that not all children like the taste.
- Make a grass face by pushing cotton wool into a section of old tights. Put the grass seed into the part where you want hair or a beard to grow. Sew the material together and cut off any excess. You can draw the face, or sew on some eyes, mouth and a nose. Dampen the grass person and then place in a saucer of water.
- Pick some flowers, leaves or twigs and create a simple arrangement with the children. Change the display from time to time.

Splashing about

Developmental focus

Children's experiences and physical skills have increased along with their vocabulary, and they can be very interested to experiment with materials in water. You can introduce words that describe the qualities of the water, such as speed of flow or temperature. Along with other abstract ideas, children will develop an understanding of these concepts. Definitely do not expect all young children to grasp and name all these ideas.

Play and learning tips

Young children learn concepts and some opposites like 'wet/dry' or 'cold/warm' because they make sense from many direct play experiences. Start the process by talking about what is happening.

Use the water tray or bowl to help children explore many different experiences with water. These play opportunities can be linked to other events, trips and observations that you make with the children. Help them to make connections.

Look at opportunities within the daily routine to use and mix water, to watch how it reacts and to mop it up.

Activities

Watery ideas

- Involve children in getting the temperature of any water just right. You might say things like, 'It's still a bit cold, isn't it? I'll add some more warm water'. Make connections to the source of the water, for example, to the hot and cold taps in your setting.
- Explore floating and sinking with a range of objects in the tray. What floats on the surface and what sinks to the bottom? What will float if it rides on something else? Is it possible to make the boat sink if you load it up too much?
- Put some ice cubes in the water and watch how they float. They can also be slid down a mini-slide into the water. (Make sure the children do not put ice cubes in their mouths.)
- Make links with other experiences: how leaves floated down the rain-filled gutter, or how, when children helped with washing, the plastic plates floated, but the metal spoons sank.

Pouring practice

- Give children plenty of experience with pouring and directing water between containers, and using waterwheels and simple pumps in the water tray.
- Use words and phrases that describe what is happening such as, the water is moving 'fast', 'slowly' or 'dribbling out very slowly'. As children fill up their containers, you can talk about 'empty', 'half full', 'full up' and 'too much' (because it is flowing over the side).
- Encourage children to fill up larger containers from smaller ones or by squeezing the water out of a sponge.
- Count out loud how many refills it takes. Let children join in if they want. Use general words such as, one container is 'big' and another is 'small', or that it took 'lots and lots' of cups to fill up the toy bucket.

Adding water

- Explore how substances change when water or a similar liquid is added. Let children be involved, or watch closely, as you blend water into various mixtures that are of practical interest to them.
- Let children help make up a new play dough batch. Explore how the dry ingredients and the water are blended into a smooth mixture that can then be used for modelling and pretend play.
- Some paint mixes need water, and you can describe the different mixes as 'too thick', 'we need some more water' or 'just right'.
- Let children watch as you use water to blend with any drink concentrates to make the right mix, or to water down the toddlers' juice. Explain simply that without the water, the drink will 'be too strong' or 'have a bad taste'.
- Explore what happens when water is added slowly to sand. Dry sand pours through their fingers, but wet sand sticks.

However, they need damp sand to make an effective sandcastle or other shape. How much water is 'just right'? If children make a very watery sand mixture in a container, can they use a fine sieve to separate out the sand from the water? Will the sand shoot through a sieve with larger holes?

Pretend play

- In the warmer weather, let children take the crockery and saucepans from the home corner outside into the garden. Provide some warm water for them to 'make tea' and 'do cooking'.
- Let children help you sweep or mop away the spillages afterwards.
- Use a small container of water set into the sand tray for children to make a pretend pond, a seaside landscape or swimming pool. They can decorate their scene with play people, boats, shells or anything else suitable.
- Give children some little shrimping nets to 'go fishing' for pretend fish, shells or any medium-sized objects in the water tray.

Natural sources of water

- Find local sources of water: a pond or stream in the park that children can enjoy with your safe involvement.
- Watch the ducks on the water, landing and taking off. Look for twigs and leaves that travel along the flow. Drop stones into the water and watch the ripples.
- Can children see themselves reflected in the water? Disturb the image with a stick and wait for it to settle.
- A local gardening centre may have little fountains or artificial water systems, and sometimes tanks of tropical fish that can enchant children.
- Explore natural water sources: watch the rain run down the windows and off the roof and draw in the condensation on the panes.
- Collect rainwater in a container and see how high up it reaches.
- Put on wellington boots and enjoy walking through puddles.

It's freezing!

- In very cold weather, show children how the water sources in the garden have frozen.
- Put out water that will freeze over night and then bring in the container and see how long it takes to melt indoors.
- Do the same activity with a container full of snow. Use words to describe the temperature like 'freezing', 'cold' and 'getting warmer'.

Travelling and learning

Developmental focus

Young children are ready to be interested and delighted by what seem like very ordinary outings to adults. What is obvious or even boring to you is often treated like a new experience by young children. Local trips can be a rich source of learning – so long as the adults view any trip through the eyes of the children. What do the children find interesting? When do they want to stop and stare? What is a sensible time for

the children? You may well organise some special trips during the year, but young children appreciate all the local trips that cost no, or very little, money.

Young children are now able to recall some of your previous outings, to talk about what they will do and later what they have seen on the trip. They will be able to walk all of a short trip, although their limited understanding of safety means they must be carefully supervised all the time.

Play and learning tips

If you are offering child care for working parents then the day can be long. Everyone needs a break and a change of scene, and young children will also benefit from learning about their local environment.

All these ideas depend on careful adult supervision that keeps children safe without unnecessarily restricting their enjoyment.

Talk with parents about what you do, and how you support early practical skills like road safety awareness.

Activities

Getting involved

- Talk with children about today's trip before you start. Make them feel involved in the plans.
- Help the children to think ahead with descriptions like, 'First we'll go to the library and get some new books. Then shall we come back past the roadworks? We can see if that big hole is still there.'
- Manage children's expectations for when it will soon be time to go. You can say, 'One more chase around the bushes, then we need to pack up.'

Reminiscing

- While you are on the trip, talk with the children about what you all see and hear. Listen carefully to what they want to say, and look at what they want to call to your attention.
- Encourage children to talk about local trips to your colleagues when you return to the nursery or to share interesting events with parents.
- Take a camera to record special events and listen to children's views on what is worthy of a photo. For example, a record of the burst water main may be just as exciting as the baby goslings.
- Make a display of the photos or any drawings that children wish to make. Lay out children's collections from a trip, such as conkers, autumn leaves or unusual rocks.

Changes over time

- Support children's ability to recall other outings with return trips to locations where

there will be continuous change.
Plan a series of trips to watch the baby ducks or other animals you see regularly, as they grow.

- Return to watch how the chestnut blossom has produced conkers, or the sycamore 'helicopters' have spiralled to the ground.
- Gardens will have flowers that mature, and perhaps vegetables like tomatoes or green beans that children can notice as they grow.
- Urban environments can generate interest in children. Return to watch the changes as the road has been dug up and gradually re-laid, or the new block of flats that is steadily being built.

Learning from travel

- Young children can safely become more active during your outings through involvement in choice of routes. They will start the process of learning to be independent local travellers.
- Offer one or two children the chance to be 'trip navigator' and let them guide the group on the familiar route to the library or the market. Help the navigators if they are uncertain and ensure that their role is enjoyable.
- Help the group to anticipate routes and landmarks with, 'Now what do you think we'll see just round this corner? Yes, it's the fire station! Let's see if the fire engines are there.'
- Take all the practical opportunities to show children how you keep them safe on the roads. Say out loud what you are doing on their behalf, and help them to be safe. You might say, 'Let's find the crossing. That's the red person, so we have to wait. Now here's the green person, so we can walk across.' If there is no pedestrian crossing, then alert children to how you look and listen and judge the safe place and time to cross the road.
- Take a short bus or train trip and show children how to buy tickets and plan a journey. Watch out for the sights, including familiar landmarks from a different angle.

Supporting pretend play

- Local trips add to children's pretend play because they can see what really happens, for example, in the train station or bank.
- Let them collect leaflets and forms that can be placed in the pretend post office area.
- Involve children in choices for shopping and let them hand over the money. They will start to understand buying, paying and getting change.

further resources

Books

Child Development from Birth to Eight, Jennie Lindon. National Children's Bureau (1993)

Listening to Four Year Olds: how they can help us plan their education and care, Jacqui Cousins. National Early Years Network (1999)

People Under Three: young children and day care, Elinor Goldschmied and Sonia Jackson. Routledge (1994)

Understanding Child Development, Thomson Learning (1998)

Young Children, Parents and Professionals: enhancing the links in early childhood, Margaret Henry. Routledge (1996)

Young Children's Close Relationships Beyond Attachment, Judy Dunn. Sage (1993)

Videos

Baby It's You. Woodside Promotions tel: 01372 805000

Communication Between Babies in Their First Year. Book and video from National Children's Bureau tel: 020 7843 6000

Heuristic Play with Objects: children of 12-20 months exploring everyday objects. National Children's Bureau

Infants at Work: babies of 6-9 months exploring everyday objects. National Children's Bureau

Tuning into Children. Book and video from National Children's Bureau